THE SON OF MAN IS THE SUPERMAN

Messiah

For

HIRE

Poems from Inner Space 1966 ~ 1982

1

BRUCE ROBERT TRAVIS

Publisher's Cataloging-in-Publication

(Provided by Quality Books, Inc.)

Travis, Bruce Robert.

Messiah for Hire: Poems From Inner Space, 1966-1982

/ by Bruce Robert Travis, - Ist ed

p. cm.

1. Love poetry, American. 2. Spirituality-Poetry.

3. Metaphysics-Poetry. 4. Reincarnation-Christianity

--Poetry.   L Title.

PS3620.R385M47 2002   813\6

QBI01-701247

ISBN: 978-0-9846731-48

December 20, 2015

"Whoever becomes highly visible as a spokesman for change gets the slings and arrows and all of the anger directed at the messenger to try to get at the message."

Vice President Al Gore
Born March 31, 1948

Bruce and Al Gore are separated by one day in age. Bruce was born April 2, 1948. Al Gore won the popular vote for the President of the United States of America.

"MESSIAH FOR HIRE"
POEMS FROM INNER SPACE
1966 -1982

Acknowledgments

I thank God for giving me the opportunity to be of service to
humanity in its time of need.

Soul reading from the Chinese Book of Oracle I Ching
November 19, 2015

I asked God the question: "Is it time yet God?" On this day I drew hexagram #24 called RETURN-THE TURNING POINT. I will summarize the reading. Unlike the three readings in *I AM BACK-HOW A SOUL REINCARNATES* there were no changing lines creating a followup reading. **"The time of darkness is past.** The winter solstice brings **the victory of light...**After a time of decay comes the turning point. **The powerful light that has been banished returns.**

There is movement but it is not brought about by force..the movement is natural arising spontaneously. For this reason **the transformation of the old becomes easy. The old is discarded and the new is introduced.** Both measures accord with the time; therefore no harm results. Societies of people sharing the same views are formed. But since these groups come together in full public knowledge and are **in harmony with the time**, all selfish separatist tendencies are excluded, and no mistake is made.

The idea of RETURN is based on the course of nature. The movement is cyclic, and the course completes itself. Therefore it is not necessary to hasten anything artificially. **Everything comes of itself at the appointed time.** This is the meaning of heaven and earth...**The firm returns.**

Things cannot be destroyed once and for all when what is above is completely split apart returns below. **Return means coming back.** (*I AM BACK*). Return is the stem of character and leads to self-knowledge. The hexagram counsels turning away from the confusion of external things, turning back to one's inner light. There, in the depths of the soul, one sees the divine, the One..To know this One means to know oneself in relation to the cosmic forces. For this One is the ascending force of life in nature and in man..**The firm is on the increase.** In the hexagram of Return one sees the mind of heaven and earth and expresses the idea that the light force is the creative principle of heaven and earth. It is an eternal cyclic movement, from which **life comes forth again just at the moment when it appears to have been completely vanquished."** *

* The *I Ching* or Book of Changes by Wilhelm/Baynes. 1969 edition.

COVER DESIGN SYMBOLISM

Messiah For Hire-Poems From Inner Space 1966-1982 chronicles the spiritual awakening process of the author in his journey into the discovery of his past life as Jesus in poetic form. This book is meant to be read in conjunction with *I Am Back -How A Soul Reincarnates.*

We have all returned to earth to learn the lessons of love. Planet earth is a correctional facility for our souls and until we learn the spiritual implication of these lessons we will keep reincarnating to earth over and over again until we get those lessons right.

The Hebrew letters between the wings translate to Y'shua or Jesus.

The *Son of Man* and the *"S"* in the center of the Star of David relates to the angelic structure of the universe as used in *Acts 7:56* in respect to Jesus as the direct descendant of King David through his second born son Nathan and the tribe of Judah. Jesus is related to the angelic hierarchy as a spiritual Son of the angel Gabri-El which means "Man of God." Thus, Jesus was the SON OF MAN of God which is why he referred to himself primarily as the Son of Man and not as the Son of God. A complete explanation of the Star of David is in *My Past Life As Jesus-An Autobiography of Two Lifetimes* pages 132 and 133. "And then the man who bears the pitcher of water will walk forth across an arc of heaven; the sign and signet of the Son of Man will stand forth in the eastern sky. The wise will lift up their heads and know that the redemption of the earth is near." *The Aquarian Gospel of Jesus the Christ of the Piscean Age* by Levi. 1895. Chapter 157:29,30.

Superman refers to the Sun's passage into the constellation of Aquarius after its precessional journey through the sign of Pisces and the rise of Christianity. Aquarius represents the up-lift-ment of hu-man as the SON OF MAN in the attainment of the Christ/love conscious spirit that dwells within us all to become children of God. *Mark 14:3* reveals this secret. Aquarius is represented by a man carrying a pitcher of water. The "Last Supper" was the **Passover** dinner describing this celestial event. Jesus was telling us when he "comes again" the Sun will have **passed over** from the constellation of Pisces into the constellation of Aquarius. With God all things are possible and we become the Superman/Hu-man. Jesus came after the Age of Aries ended. Aries is the I AM of the zodiac signs and represented by the ram/lamb. Jesus was considered the "great shepherd."

Messiah For Hire: We are all here NOW in the Age of Aquarius to save ourselves and then empower others with truth and unconditional love. It's our job. We are all the Messiah. Collectively humanity can save itself.

The *Wings of Hope* represent our up-lift-ment, ascension and transcendence to our higher soul self and the "Kingdom of God" which is eternal life and not having to reincarnate to earth anymore unless it is voluntary. The "Kingdom of Heaven" is not the final destination. It is another material dimension.

The *Interlocking Triangles of the Star of David* symbolizes this process. The lower triangle represents the soul imprisoned in the material worlds of illusion and duality. When the soul turns towards God and to unconditional Love the upper triangle representing this up-lift-ment of the higher self raises the lower self with it on the *Wings of Hope.*

The *Horns* of the Aries ram, the I AM as the sacrificial lamb spoken of by the prophet Isaiah. Jesus said, "Before Abraham was I AM" establishing his identity and Oneness with the Father/God.

The *Cornucopia* is the abundance, the fullness that is Christ/ Love, that is God, because Love brings Completeness, Oneness, Inter-connectedness and Unity.

The *Arabic letters* below *Poems From Inner Space-1966-1982* are from the *Koran Surah XLII 13*. The entire verse reads: "He hath **ordained** for you that religion which he **commanded** unto Noah, and that which we **inspire** in thee [Muhammad] and that which we **commended** unto Abraham and Moses and Jesus, saying, Establish the religion and BE NOT DIVIDED THEREIN."

HEART OF LIGHT- Behind the letters of Messiah and the double SS with the emanating rays of light is the Heart of Light. It is very subtle. Behind the SS is the heart center of the universe, which is God, which is Love. This "place" is called the Kingdom of God. This Center represents the Christ Consciousness inherent and lying dormant in every human being. The Center is the 6th gate on the Qabalistic Tree of Life and is the Tiphareth or human consciousness of our Divine Self represented by the Sun of our solar system. Light and Consciousness are the basic ingredients of Creation.

The key to world peace and unity is the recognition that we are all inter-connected in the universe and that we are One humanity. One human race. God "ordained" for Muhammad to "establish the religion" of Unity and for humanity to "be not divided." There can be no unity when there is division. Any true Muslim must follow the word of God to their prophet. God is clear. The "religion" God "ordained" for Muhammad is the same one that he "commanded unto Noah" and "commended unto Abraham, Moses and Jesus."

I encourage the reader to look up the definitions of the words bolded above for a better understanding of what God was instructing Muhammad to do. I will give the definition of the most important one, "ORDAINED" which means "confer holy orders upon, to enact or establish by law or edict; to decree." How can any true Muslim go against that which God "ordained" for Muhammad? This puts all true Muslims, Jews and Christians, in fact, all of humanity in a unique position. Which God do you pledge your allegiance to? The God of darkness, violence, terror, hatred, death and division? Or the God of Love, Light, Unity and Oneness? Since God "ordained" the "holy order" upon Muhammad all true Muslims must abide by that holy decree. It cannot be otherwise.

To whom you pledge your allegiance is resolved in the *New Testament* Book of *John 8:44,45* if you do not choose the God of Love, Oneness and Light. Jesus says: "You belong to your father the devil, and you want to carry out your father's desires. He was a murderer from the beginning, not holding to the truth, for there is no truth in him. When he lies, he speaks his native language, for he is a liar and the father of lies. And because I tell you the truth, you believe me not." The choice is clear. Jesus made it clear. "If you are not with me you are against me."

John 8:42,43. "If God were your Father, you would love me, for I proceeded forth and have come from God. For I have not even come on my own initiative, but He sent me. Why do you not understand what I am saying? **It is because you cannot hear my word.**" "...That which we inspire in thee Muhammad and that which we commended unto Abraham and Moses and Jesus."

"BE NOT DIVIDED..."

15

Miami International Airport
October 22, 2015

CHRIST-MAS = LOVE MORE

LOVE IS THE KEY

POEMS FROM INNER SPACE
1966 to 1982

I Dreamed of Peace (song) - 1966

In their blindness they can only see
all the hatred and animosity:
but I wasn't blind and I could clearly see
all that existed was hypocrisy.
Then I took a trip... all the world seemed good;
I saw the world in peace and brotherhood,
but I wasn't blind and could clearly see
all that existed was hypocrisy.

Breaking Through (song) - 1967

Sitting in my mind's crowded corridor

My embryonic journey to my being...

Engulfed in the tissues and the currents of my thoughts,

I'm left to be alone with me.

I'm afraid of myself and the weakness of my mind

I've lost my way... I've lost reality.

Will I ever get back... will I ever find my way?

I've lost my mind... I've lost my sanity!

The passageways are dark. There is no light to see.

I'm searching for some signs of liberty –

I value my freedom, but I love my peace of mind

That comes from love, that stems from security.

I think I've found myself; I believe I know my kind.

I will never lose myself in the confines of my mind...

The long hard journey's ended and the light is bright to see

I'm reaching out to someone... come share my life

with me!

**Dedicated to Hunter Leggett - From his resignation letter
to the Unitarian Church - 1969**

I valued and cherished the friendship of six years
of those I've known and grown to love in grief, in want, in
cheer;
a monument of meaning, accomplishments in time;
because of love and family needs, by these I must resign.
The making of the parting, a decision hard to make,
a force so strong reflecting wants, by these I must relate.
I ask for your forgiveness and understanding too
I have my pride for things I've done in love, in want, in truth.
The guilt I have with you I'll share, for I am not to blame,
but share with me my feelings of a better state of change.
So give your love and faith and hope to that monument of
mine,
and with it grow in love and peace to share with all mankind.

I Came Into the Universe - March 1971

I came into the Universe so powerful and strong
like a fury smashing through fields of blue and seas of green,
by a force that ruled and controlled my love and captured my
soul
all at once like a whirlpool of rapture leading me to a world
never seen before; drowned, but not lost, in love
my feelings once again restored.

Being sucked into the whirling, swirling fury of tortuous love
I was reaching the end, like the gyrating top about to topple.

Almost there, I saw white stars on black in the cold emptiness
of space,
yet the sun's warmth reflected in my gaze and left me warm.
Quickly now, a thunderous pace, rising tides –
Oh God
You do exist, but in the womb of wondrous love.

It was then, I came into the Universe,

Maniacal Ragings – 1971

Maniacal ragings... when will it end?
The world's damned crazy, but it's always been:
We must accept that as life -
Love *is* ***God***
And that is something attainable for
forever anyway.

Compared to Antiquity - Summer 1971

Compared to antiquity

my first segment is but a grain of sand on an endless beach

reaching into a vast never-ending sea of forgotten memories.

At Melvin's - 1971

Railing culture overlooking countless stares
of looking for something somethings.
Incandescent hues of white bright lobes
on searching souls staring out into night's stifled sounds:
Choking not, but breathing life's life-styles.

Nature 's green shrouds earthen flesh
Helpless, seemingly helpless, in the throes
of innocence prevailing in the world.
Evil abounds so strong, but God's gentle touch
emanates love into our world of woe,
Overcoming the evil hapless menacing
the very existence of our souls.
Only the happy, carefree souls
knowing not what transpires in this life
shall go forth fearless, head-long into life's endless oblivion.

Unfinished Ode to a Water Fountain - Summer 1971

Seemingly silent crescendos that never reach their peak,

audible only to those who happen to be walking by;

recognized most by small children

who make their otherwise dull existence an exciting

happening,

enabled by pushing fingers and thumbs, to escape the

inevitable –

that which we, too, must realize.

A Myriad of Gold — September 1971

A Myriad of gold reflected in the grey and damp September
night
Faintly glowing, suspended like dying suns in twilight hour;
A borning, but not quite warmth in my glowing heart -
What I feel is like a child's joy of a new and wondrous thing...
Contained not, for a joy is a short-lived lifetime
of a feeling felt now.

Foraging Through World's Travails - 1972

Foraging through world's travails
I can't bring myself to face
the simplistic obstacles of mundane everyday existence;
It seems futile that at such an early age
I worry about my end
that seems infinitesimal yet miniscule
compared to the passage of Time...
Worry not, dear friend,
for your passage shall endure forever.

Life is Too Soon to Tell - 1972

Life is too soon to tell.

Sunny Skies (song) – *Mexico, Fall of 1971*

Sunny skies shining their light on me
thinking of you I clearly see
the joy and the happiness that can be
shared between us forever.

Can you imagine the times to be had
our moments together both happy and sad...
Oh, Can't you see us, can't you see us
being together, forever?

My soul is glowing, my eyes are smiling:
my heart is filled with the love I am trying
to hide from you... it's too soon to show you.
what I'm feeling it's real.

And we'll walk along the sands of time.
We'll count our moments and we'll count our times
of the days past and nights gone by
our moments that were shared together.
And those sunny skies will shine their light on me
I'll think of you and I'll clearly see
the joy and the happiness that will be
shared between us together... forever.

Know From Whence You Come... and Where You Shall Go
-

August 1972

Flowing forward like a newly formed stream
Pressing further on led only in the direction by the force
By which you are ruled, you know not by which path
Or direction you shall go; but you go hoping
That your churning, swirling desires lead you not endless
But into a vast beautiful open sea of everything you hoped life
to be.

The storm shall subside, the flood waters will ebb
And only a twinkle of a seemingly tempestuous past
Shall, too, erode into oblivion.
New rivers form and waves are made
Some... like gentle rolls on a windless pond
Others like the mountainous fury of an angry sea.

ONLY WE
ARE OUR
OWN VAST OCEANS.
WE... SHAPE... AND FORM
OUR DESTINIES.

WE... FORGE... LIFE'S DAMS... WE... CAN... CONTROL
THOSE
THUNDEROUS WAVES
Or make gentle ripples... IT IS OUR CHOOSING.

Guide that rushing torrent
But guide it gently...

FOLLOW ITS NATURAL COURSE... but...
Observe its direction.

KNOW FROM WHENCE YOU COME... AND WHERE
YOU SHALL GO.

If I Had But One Love - 1972

If I had but one love to spend in my whole entire life
I would spend it on you.
Most loves, like lovers, diminish in time
like a vanishing species.
And love today seems to diminish as does the
passage of time.
If I had but one love to spend in my whole entire life
I would spend it on you.
I would be like Scrooge or Howard Hughes
I would treasure my love but I would never
give it up...
Spend it? Yes! Spend it all, give it away
to you!
If I had but one love to spend in my whole entire life
I would spend it all... on you.

My Love For You -

September 29, 1972 7:50 P.M.

My love for you is like
bagels, lox and cream cheese.
If I have it, I want to have the whole thing,
and not have a part of you separate from the rest.

Dishes

Fall 1972

I WISH you WOULDN'T
You KNOW you SHOULDN'T
And it would be my wishes
If you DIDN'T do
My GODDAMN DISHES!

A Gentle Splash of Spring

1972

It came like the ferocity of a violent storm
a thunderbolt striking the first recognizable
yet unidentifiable object...
Seeking out the proverbial "needle in the haystack"
the storm was felt.
Then the rains came and it was like all the world
was pouring from my soul into a warm earth
that acted as my loving receptacle -
My storming fury will never harm you
as a flash flood does leaving victims in its wake.
My aftermath is a gentle splash of spring
with an obvious trail of tell-tale love.

Looking in Your Eyes

September 20, 1972

Looking in your eyes...
Images mirrored reflected in my gaze;
Confusion sets the pace, yet peace is just around the comer -
Let yourself go... fly with the breeze.

I see myself some time ago-
lost… no way out... like a mouse in a maze:
I know the way - follow me,
we won't get lost... we won't get lost.

You Make the Sun Shine in My Heart

September 12. 1972

You make the sun shine in my heart
when the clouds hide the bright rays
and I'm kept warm by my thoughts of you.

Leave Your Blues Behind (song) - 1972

How I pictured you envisioned in my mind

a faint recall of beauty… who's that girl, what's her name?

I'd like to get to know her I need someone to love

she looks damn good and I'm alone. I'd take her if 1 could.

So come out today, Baby,

leave your blues behind

forget the things that made you sad

and play with me a while.

I'll help you to forget the past and send bad thoughts away;

the time for you to change has come

the time is here today.

I'd like to get to know you, something keeps us apart

it makes me sad knowing you're alone

come on, let's make a start.

CHORUS

We've been together ten long weeks

we've had our ups and downs,

we laugh and love most all the time.

yet still you always frown,

you take life so damned seriously and not let live today,

the time for you to change has come...

the time is here today.

CHORUS

That Which

April, 1973

That which is beautiful is not necessarily
that which is real and what we see;
that which is real is not necessarily beautiful
but that which we perceive;
that which we perceive is not necessarily beautiful or real
and that which is
is not necessarily real at all.

I Would Sooner Be Late

1973

I would sooner be late and be remembered
than to have been on time and been forgotten.*

* And, behold, there are last which shall be first, and there are
first which
shall be last. *Luke 13:30*

I Mean… What the Fuck! – 1973

I mean… what the fuck!!!

Possessed February 1973

A possessive man I am not.

And I thought I to have a mind as wide as a sea

Stretched between two shores

And as deep as the deepest sea is deep.

But... I have neither

And I am shocked by the sudden frailty

And child-like weakness of a jealous mind.

Possessed by selfish thoughts of denial

From what I love most.

Obsessed by the thought of rage

At whom?... At Myself.

For WHO AM I to possess THAT WHICH I have not.

And be obsessed by THAT WHICH is not.

Where Our Love Grows

April. 1973

Supposing we liken the growing of a garden to the rake and
hoe
and to the movement of our legs to our feet and toes;
a garden of love has special seeds to grow
and the implements and conditions for sowing is the love 1
have for you.
No rakes or hoes in my tender garden growing;
only love, sweet caress and tenderness are spawning this
budding love
that's growing -
for you. my sweet our love will grow;
spring's sweet rains and warm earth glowing, sun's gentle rays,
soft
breezes blowing
shall kiss this place where our love grows...
in my garden of love where our love grows.

Reflections of a Childhood Past

April. 1973

I'm saddened by the realization that only in my fading
thoughts can I go back;
I forget most, but if I pry hard enough, I can unseal and let
escape
enough of the past to make me laugh with anger and cry with
delight.
At 25 my fleeting mind is as stable as a child's;
Who was I when 1 was 5? Was I me?
Or at 6, 7, or 8? - was I loved as a child should be loved?
I'm sure I was... or was I?
I was cared for and fed, had warm clean clothes to wear,
but was I loved for being me?
If love existed I would be what I was, for that is love -
letting me be what I was.

Number 54

June 4, 1973

I try to love, but I try too hard… it seems that way, you make
me believe it so.

At an age as mine, I cannot love too much and feel it wrong.

I try to love but you take it not saying, "Hug me close, but let
me go."

My passion is my torment and my love seems to dig its own
grave deeper.

My headstone shall be inscribed:

"Here lies a man who loved too much,

and at such an early age. his passion laid to rest

for one who truly loved but loved too much."

Away with fatal thoughts and scorn for myself;

my love shall never die. for a blazing star shall not be doused
by feeble rain.

Raise yourself up: the love you have as strong as this
is a sacred love not often found.

Feel sorry not that your fire always burns for the one you love;

be scorned not that your woman feels not that torch which
burns

within your heart at every meeting.

Love and affection are the keys to the lock opening the door

and become the principles of union, the essential key to

relatedness for all

mankind.

And most of all, an affection sparked by no previous plans or

premeditation;

spontaneous combustion is the zenith, the paramount

combination for the

perfect union.

The Twin Star

July 23, 1973- 3:30 A.M.

Looking for the twin star may just well take me
To eternity
And that profound revelation that my perfection
My twin star
May be disguised in the image of a flowering earth
And not in the robes of a blazing sun.
Need my fire rage fiercer by another consumed
In flame?
Why this belief of a twin star?
A life consumed in endless flame, a raging fire
Fed by other fire and the air, which too,
It also feeds.
A well kindled fire can be contained by earth
And water and still burn as hot and bright
Without harming that which surrounds it...
Earth and water so too receive from the
Guiding light of the Flame, the warmth from
Its fire.
So do not believe the thought and the false

Guiding light of others, that peace shall be
Found in one as thyself and in no other.
The twin star we seek is not the image of me
But dressed in the guise of some other.

Distance Makes No Matter - October 6, 1973

Why can't we spend our time alone
together, apart?
Distance makes no matter!
And, in true love, absence makes the
Heart grow fonder...
I know that now.

The two that we are apart
have a right to be ONE in love,
And the ONE that we are,
Has a right to remain two... in love.
Yet still apart,
I see that now.
Distance makes no matter!

The inner peace that comes from
Being alone as ONE is most beautiful.
But the inner peace that comes from
Being alone as two is most divine
I feel that now.
Distance makes no matter!

My Night Is Dawning - October 7. 1973

It takes time to see the light of day
Adjustment to see the black of night
But the night comes and so brings forth
Another day -

MY NIGHT IS DAWNING and the light of day
Shows me the path to follow out of
The black of night...

I see things now by the light of day
That I could not see in the black of night.

The Ultimate Contest - November, 1973

Individual self expression, an assertion of one's being,
To establish identity and obviate anonymity, For whom?
For ourselves. For doing so we establish ourselves in
such a manner that we become worthwhile to others in the
process; thus this one to one cycle reinforces itself.

Being able to "cope" so to speak with one's self and this
new found self expression, we are ready for the ultimate
contest: maintaining the sacred and inviolable individual
self-expression in a man woman relationship,
a compatibility on all levels.
Spiritual, mental, physical and sexual. All paramount
for a peaceful and meaningful co-existence. A beautiful
relationship
is one of calm and tranquility spiced with the exhilaration
of doing things together, or apart, never losing that
self-expression or identity and not feeling
separate or apart when not together.
The ultimate joy of doing things with one you love.

Somehow I Just See - January 11, 1974, 1:40 A.M.

Somehow I just see,

I don't know why

It's easy for me

No great gift.

Just a feeling.

I feel.

It's nice to feel

It makes me free

It sets me apart from myself

And at times

I'm just standing there

Staring at myself

And it's nice

To get away

Once in a while.

My Mind is Streaking - March 10. 1974, 1:30 A.M.

My mind is streaking

what a relief

to have shed

my cocoon

I've metamorphosed

into my naked self

no longer clothed

in the robes

of linen insecurities

I too shall dance free

like a butterfly

skating on the sky

dancing on the clouds

and being free

with the hope

that some day

the butterflies that we are

will have a right... to be.

Radiance From Without and From Within

August 1, 1974- 1:08 A.M.

A radiance from without

And from within.

This one's for us.

Energy?

There is more than meets the eye.

We can only see what we want

And

We can only see what we want to see.

Why, when it's right in front of us

Are we blind to the most obvious?

Aloneness Cannot Be Said to Be Loneliness

August 2, 1974

It is better to be ONE
And alone.

Than to be two
And unhappy.

Aloneness cannot be said to be loneliness...

At Least A Thousand Lives Before -

December 2, 1974, 5:00 A.M.

At least a thousand lives before!
Yet today, we've met, not the first time.
Since time and space do not exist
I'm sure we've known each other before.

And here we are, no difference, not apart
United once again; this time, maybe
The last time... it does not matter –
We're here now.

Disharmony Is the Root of All Our Evils - December 7, 1974

I say to you that I AM GOD
And so too are you
If you so choose to be.
WE ARE the power
And the glory!
When WE shine
GOD shines
When we shine…
WE ARE the universal ALL-In-ALL.
God, our Father, is that extreme power
Of intelligence and force
That dwells in us all.
The force for good
That knows no evil.
The force for truth
That is
Universal truth.
To BECOME one with GOD
We must first fall into harmony
And BECOME one with OURSELVES
To become united with God
With ourselves,
We must unite again
In perfect harmony.
So what is evil?
Anything that is
Not in harmony.
Being one with God
Birds sing, the heavens ring
And we soon learn the most obvious of all

The cosmic truths.
Disharmony is the
Root Of All Our Evils.

Wake Up - December 9. 1974, Mexicana Airlines

WAKE UP!
Your are falling down. Uh oh. watch out.
Too late. You hurt yourself... that's too bad
You're down, might as well enjoy the pain
Because that is what you are conscious of now.
The pain.
It hurts. I know.
It's very real.

WAKE UP!

Enjoy that pain, understand why you fell.
Oh, you weren't paying attention.
You mean you were unconscious.
I was awake!!
Then why did you fall?
Because I wasn't paying attention.
You mean you were unconscious.

WAKE UP!

It seems the first thing you do
When you wake up is become unconscious.
How absurd this must sound.
But it's true.
When you wake up the first thing to do
Is wake up. I'm awake. I'm alive. I'm conscious.

WAKE UP!

Be like the gyrating whirling maple SEED
Falling
To
The
Earth.
We have a purpose, a function.
A duty to perform.
We are the seeds.
And seeds must grow.
As we grow, our duty performed
Our mission accomplished
To give other seeds.

WAKE UP!

There are thousands of other seeds
Floating
Down
With
You,
But only one, maybe two
Maybe none at all
Will
Get
Down
To the business of living.
The seed is not enough.
It will not become realized
Or noticed
IN THIS WORLD
Until it is a tree.
Simple, isn't it?
Pay attention.

WAKE UP?

We are all seeds
Floating
Down.
But most of us just lie... Dormant.
Never growing and
RETURN TO THE EARTH
We're born, we die.
We return to the source
From... which... we... came.
Never realized, our duty, our purpose.
Not fulfilled.
Well, maybe NEXT TIME.
Next time?
What did you say?
-I said,

WAKE UP!

We get another chance.
We're born. we die
but
We are like the seed from the tree.

61

Many are born.
But only a few grow.
Such an abundance from nature.
Even a surplus.
Possibly a waste.
But only a glimmer of possibility.
What did you say? I said.

WAKE UP!

Pay attention.
To become the tree
You must first realize
That you are first the seed
And
That
You
Are
Falling.
Before you reach earth you know your mission.

WAKE UP

It's not too late.
Open your eyes
Your falling fast
Spinning out of control.
Oh my God!
I'm going to... Die.
Don't worry son.
You are already dead!

WAKE UP!

Man is born and re-born.
And never really grows.
But. the possibility to grow is there.
Nature gives to man.
We must make an effort.
Staying awake all the time
is an effort.
But look at the reward.

If you were awake
You
Would
Never
Have
Fallen.

WAKE UP!

WAKE UP!

The Awakening - December 19, 1974 10:30 A. M.

The whole process of realization or the reality of understanding
or the understanding of reality. The "awakening" is like a
vast whirlpool. Once inside we are pulled closer and
closer to the center, and soon the centrifugal
force becomes so strong it is impossible to
turn back. Each gyration closer to the
center is like a stage of develop-
ment; each step along the way,
this spinning towards the
center is the one con-
stant in life. Change.
This change
is the moment,
the now.

Being part of the whirlpool and its motion is this constant we
call change. This change is reality. Knowing this we become
more aware, thus becoming more conscious; this
whirlpool leads us to the center which is
understanding. When one gets to the center
one understands; thus we can see that at the
center of the whirlpool, which some call
the end, is the constant moment,
constant experience. Understanding
coupled with experience is the
action of consciousness,
realization,
reality.

When we get to the center of the whirlpool
we can say we have returned to the center
of our "Being," both as our existence
and our existence in relation
to life as a constant
conscious experience

a life of knowing, of
understanding.

At the Beginning - December 20, 1974

Living, a raga, flowing up and
down.
Spontaneous, alive,
Explosions in sound...abound...
In being
In knowing
In understanding.
Men understand not the abstract
which is the ultimate expression.
Oneness of being
at the moment
knowing,
understanding
living.
We are forever seeking and we always seem
To finish... at the beginning...
Only to start our seeking
Once again
at the beginning.
Maybe there is something to the beginning
We always wind up there after each leaving.
I'm home now.
Once again,
this time for good.
I've been set free.
It's funny, I never really left.
I was here all the time
and never knew it.
This knowing, this understanding.
Such freedom... no seeking.
Reality
Living
The most beautiful raga of them all.

Life is a "Mis" Understanding - December 23, 1974, 11:30 A.M.

LIFE, is a "miss" understanding... and somehow

we keep missing the point.

We're born, we die,

For most, a one way ticket to the grave.

It's sad, it really is.

People 'Live' a whole life never really knowing

What it is to truly understand.

One foot in the past,

One foot in the future.

No feet left for the present.

A race of 'Living' non-existence!

What is it that really exists?

I'll tell you! - What time is it?

THE TIME IS NOW!

That which really is.

Once you realize this

You are on your way

To... understanding.

Now, I'll make my point.

The only CONSTANT

In life is... CHANGE

...ETERNAL CHANGE

LIFE is now a continuous one way ticket

To... being.

And, "BEING " IS the only way to LIVING

Love is the Key (song) - 1974

Understanding is the key to living
Rest your love inside of your heart
Come Outside of yourself for a while
To see you've been living in the dark.

Once you've seen the light you've been forgiven
Turning back's the wrong thing to do
Set your sights upon the mountain of Love
And everything will be all right to choose.

Love is the key
Understand Me.

Being here and now is the best thing
Then love is such an easy thing to do
Open up your heart let yourself enter through
Because happiness will be inside for you.

You've found yourself and everything's worth living
The Sun still shines even on cloudy days
You've seen the light and you'll sure spread THE NEWS
Cause loving is the only thing to do.

Love is the key
Understand Me.

Now we go to conscious understanding
Aware of almost everything you do
Enter in take a look at yourself
What dwells inside is peace and love for you.

Christmas Eve Reflections - 1974, 11:15 P.M.

What a cosmic joke.

I search and search looking

For some answers.

Here I am, alone, at Harlow's

A nightclub, the center of it

All, so they say.

We're closed.

No Christmas trees, no tinsel.

Not strings of popcorn,

Just these thoughts

And myself.

The answer IS here.

Just live friend.

One day at a time.

Moment by moment,

Hang on.

You're almost there.

Where?

Here! ...confused?

Yes, a little... why?

I mean, what's it all about?

A woman? Yes, maybe

I'm ready to share

My secrets... and laugh... once again.

I just love cosmic jokes.

Ralph, The Resident Snail - January 2, 1975

Ralph, the resident snail
knows not where it's at
2,000 miles traveling,
not by his choice or will I'm sure.
Wrapped and insulated in aluminum over-wear,
on a verdant carriage of green,
tourist class, ticket free,
from the lowlands
to the summit.

South to north, east to west,
It's all the same;
Now -
Ralph's here, he's cool, he's a snail.
Traveling, now unraveling,
he's here
not by choice, not by will,
but by his fate
that he's a snail.
Not in control, "let the chips fall where they may."
Most of us, at one time,
are like Ralph,
a third class letter
lost in the mail,
and the chances are slim that we'll be found.

Cast off your shell,
be like the boat
on the wind,
and sail, sail, sail.

Matter - January 3, 1975

One... solitary... ray... of... sunlight
Beaming through a tightly knit blanket of clouds.
Life, as we know it.
A reflection in reverse
Luminous shafts of light we are
Trying to penetrate inwards
As if upwards through the earthly
Mire of materialism and desire
That clouds our way.

To get within, to the light source.
We must go without,
To get back in.
It is not the giving up that matters.
That does not matter.
What is the matter
Is being controlled
By matter.
When it doesn't matter
All this matter
Then it matters.

Take the reins and take control
The path forward leads to light
The tunnel is long and dark.
Keep your eyes trained
On that speck of light
In the far distance
And don't look back.

What Has a Beginning Must Have and End - January 12. 1975

Loving God is to know God.
Knowing God is loving others.
Loving others is knowing thyself.
In knowing and loving thyself
We pay the highest tribute to God,

Denying God is to know nothing
Disbelief in God breeds disbelief in others
Believing in nothing is not believing in self.
Denying self is denying existence exists.

Not believing is to deny loving
Not loving is denying existence.
Denying life.
No longer living we slip on the cloak
Of eternal night and loneliness
And partake of the elixir that
Destroys the soul.

By denying the existence of God
We deny the existence of ourselves.
By denying the existence of ourselves.
We cease to be,
We are... alone... absolute loneliness.
By ceasing to be.
We can only float eternally alone
In the coal black vacuum of space.
What has a beginning must have an end.
But how long is eternity?
And where does infinity end?

Reflections of Like Mind and Soul (song for guitar and orchestra)

February 2. 1975

Looking in your eyes I see calmness and serenity
Reflections of like mind and soul
It's love I see, you've told me so.

Speak no words, you speak my mind
We'll sit entranced
Our souls combined
In love we'll be
T 'was meant to be
Sojourning thru eternity.

Oh... Oh... Oh...

(Break)
We've met again just like before
2,000 years or maybe more
The times we've lived being apart
Hold my hands, take my heart.
We'll travel on to far away places
The sun will set into our faces
Sending down a million rays of sunlight
It's bright, the light, new sight
Oh... Oh... Oh...

(Break)
Yes. I see the light it's bright enough to find
The path that leads into our minds
Sending down a million rays of sunlight
It's bright, the light, new sight,

(Repeat first verse)

Hello... Nice to Know You Once Again - February 4, 1975, 12:30 a.m.

So! It has been spoken.
There are many ways and words.
That puts one on the path
That leads to the light.
Love! There is nothing more sacred and divine.
The communion of two souls fulfills
the mission.
Two halves to make a whole,
As left is to right,
As day is to night.
One's reflection in the
Stillness of a pond.
Yin and Yang!
Cause and effect.

All love.
A reminder of God's constant presence.
Love!
Perfect balance.
Harmony
The coming together of the universal principles
Love!
A thought
A force.
An ideal.

Elise
That radiance shining light and love
And warmth.
A lot like the sun.
A lot like me.
Like souls do attract.
Hello... nice to know you once again.

In The Desert - February 4, 1975

Sitting,

Alone

I

Listen

to the

Silence and the Quietude

And Silence became the ultimate

sound of all.

In

Silence,

One

Hears

Everything

TRILOGY FOR ELISE

Night Flight to Tucson - February 6. 1975. 1:20 A.M..

Say it chance our first breaths
Were drawn at the same source?
And say it chance
On the night of our meeting
The race had run its course?
No, not quite yet.

I thought last chance
Or was it fat chance
That I could meet you

Someway, somehow,
The question was... when?
Why not tomorrow,
On a night flight to Tucson.
Ah! I can see it now...
Lovers meet,
Romance over Oklahoma City.
But wait
One small problem,
Who made all those arrangements?

I didn't think that,
I just wrote it now,
I hardly knew your name.

And... there you were.
The object of my thoughts,
On a night flight to Tucson.
"Fancy meeting you here."
Chance?

Ha!
I can only smile.

Don't Speak It's Understood - February 6. 1975, 1:55 A.M.

It's very funny

Sitting here thinking of you.

I'm smiling!

I'm looking into your eyes

And I can laugh.

Don't speak. It's understood.

Your there.

I'm here.

It does not matter.

That sparkle in your eye.

Like a child's.

Take my hands and we will lead each other.

Look into my eyes.

What do you see?

A reflection of yourself?

Yes, there are two ways to take that.

The secret echoes throughout the universe.

It is no secret.

Don't speak, it's understood.

How Does One Measure Time? - February 6, 1975, 2:35
A.M.

How does one measure time?
I'll put mine in a spoon.
It fits nicely there.
All of eternity wouldn't even fill a glass.
Time? Try to grasp it...
Better yet, catch your shadow.
How does one understand something that does not exist?
Easy!
Understand its non-existence.
And existence becomes relative to it.
What's relative?
Nothing, really!
Life just is.
And that is everything.
Relating to no one thing,
Just being a part of it all.

How does one measure Love?
I'II put mine in the infinite universe.
It fits nicely there,
And even then it would overflow.
Love? Take hold of it.
Better yet, take hold of yourself and
Look within.
How does one understand something that is everything?
Easy!
Understand its total existence and experience.
And existence becomes relative to it.
What's relative?
Everything really!
That is life.

Relating to everything,
Not being a part of any one thing.

You've Got My Heart - February 13, 1975, 1:40 A.M.

You've got my
heart. What more could I
ask for except that I have yours
in return. Some give this or that,
I give you that which is holy –
my spirit to join yours.
Let us join our forces and
power and conquer
the world
together.

Go Gently Into the Forest - February 27, 1975, 4:00 A.M.

Go

gently into the forest. Step

lightly and do not make a sound. For

the snapping of one twig shall reverberate

around the world. I have found with you

the peace of fields and streams flowing

through me, a continuous rush of love.

Only the animals could understand

What I feel. For

lacking in

logic and

reason.

only

what is

true to the

senses makes

sense at all.

Only that which

abounds in the

small of my heart.

There is a River - February 17, 1975, 4:45 A.M.

There is a river
That has no beginning
And no end.
There is a force
That has no bounds
Makes no amends.
There is an intelligence
That knows it all
And with it sends
Total love
That makes you my sister
Makes you my friend.
For All Are One and
One Is All.
Flow back to the Source
And... heed the call.

I'm Kissed By Your Presence - March 9, 1975

Lord

I'm kissed by your presence

I'm blessed by your smile

Too Much Is Not Enough - April 29, 1975, Harlow's, 10:56
P.M.

Stillness? No a longing –

I am impatient for your constant love,

I cannot be with you enough.

Too much is not enough.

Joy can not be fulfilled without you.

Love can not be if you are absent from

My heart.

Still my quivering soul, yet quicken

My spirit.

My life began when we met.

The Love Junkie - February 14, 1976, Valentine's Day

The Prince of Peace is here to stay
make no mistake about it.
My Love for you is so damn strong
I cannot live without it.
It's like a drug, I'll need a fix,
Each day and then forever,
A shot of Love each day for life
From that I'll never sever
"He's the Love Junkie," they'll whisper,
Shot up, strung out, a mainline through his veins
His Love's the stuff, the high's the best,
It's rushing to his brains.
What a rush, I'm hooked for life
There's nothing to replace it.
The Junkie of Love, I'm flying high
This time I know I'm wasted.

The Wedding - February, 1976

Ah, the indwelling spirit manifests in the
Temple of flesh.
T'is the wedding of love supreme and
Intellect sublime that wisdom be born.
The resultant son is the light and
Sheds his radiance upon thee.

It's Love! Cheers! I'll Drink to That - January 14, 1976

It's the glittering of the diamond

The facets are us all.

Perfection paramount tri-angled.

The power in us all.

Look into the diamond.

What is it that you see?

Perfection in reflection?

Yes! The love I have for thee.

The Love is One, the One is All.

It's All the same to me.

"No" matter how I cut the ice

One in the same, the same in one

The One in us all. "Who" cares anyway?

It's Love! Cheers; I'll drink to that.

To the occasion?

Let's have a ball.

Messiah For Hire - March 1 1976, 1:30 A.M.

He's in training you know, his stars told him so
To teach, to love, and to counsel.
The sacrificial lamb, has returned to this land
To destroy what has caused her to sin so.

This world's lost her way in deepening decay
Her powers have all become rivals.
Only eight years more to even the score
Or Armageddon will surely survive us.

We've still got the time to balance this rhyme
With logic. with love, and with reason
To even the score we've got to love more
Or the Lord will condemn us for treason.

I've Borne My Cross Long Enough - April 22, 1976

I've borne my cross long enough, I cannot hang around
The thorns are digging deeper and I've seemed to lost
My crown

The pain and the suffering, the last things I shall feel
I've been betrayed, I'm all alone
It all seems so unreal.

My love's not enough, nor my understanding, too
You've stripped me of my birthright
You mock me,
Oh you fools.

So, I'd better make my exit, I'd better soon expire
For Gods on hand to take my love, to take me
Up much higher.

But I say to you and I make this vow
I'll tell you why they made me die
I knew the truth and they knew lies
The people loved but they despised
The things I know I'll tell you now
It's in the stars
I'll show you how
I'll show you how.

It's prophesied I shall return
It's written in the holy word
I've been reborn I'll love again
The Christ is here, the Christ
Within
The Christ is love,

Each man in himself has God within his heart
To start again, be born anew
You've got to make a start
You've got to make a start.

Love Is Surely The King - August 16, 1976, 9:00 A.M.

The 28th of July marked a time in the sky

A very auspicious occasion.

The Sun and the Moon, Venus and Mercury too.

and Saturn all in liaison.

Here's what it means

Begin listening

To the words

To the rhyme

To the reason

The Christ has arrived delivered on time

To begin a new type of season

He is 28 now and wants to show how

This world can laugh, and Love and sing

The Christ* has arrived,

And Christ is the Love And Love is surely the King.

* "...For one thing, we must acknowledge that when the document refers to Christ it does not mean Jesus, as we have pointed out in a previous chapter, the word that in English we pronounce Christ, is a translation of the Greek word Christos, which in turn is a translation of the Hebrew word that we call Messiah. As we have previously emphasized, the word is not the name of a person but the title of an office..."

The Meaning of The Dead Sea Scrolls by A. Powell Davies. p. 103. 1956

The Great Cosmic Plan - June 7, 1978, 9:30 a. m.

Things were fine in the garden at Eden
Loving life, walking naked and doing no thinking:

But Adam got taken by Eve's picking and eating
So their time in the garden would soon be a fleeting.

So their first evil deed caused a change in the speed
Of God's plan for the earth's redemption,
A new thought in his mind to bind up in time

So here will I make of its mention;
A new MASTER PLAN soon devised by the man
ADAM KADMON
To whom we owe our creation
With a quick zip and a zap a bim and a bang
A new thought for man's re-elevation.

YOU SEE?

Adam fell from his grace and must return to this place
We call the Garden of Eden

Where dwells peace of mind and where lovers are kind.
And where no races are running for freedom.

SO!

A MESSIAH was needed and there was only ONE

To whom it was deeded

The blueprint to this new master plan

Look to the stars to Venus and Mars.

It is there... The great COSMIC PLAN

READ

Revelation twenty two sixteen

The great clue to this scheme

For the ROOT and OFFSPRING of David.

The BRIGHT and MORNING STAR is Venus, not Mars

And reincarnation is the key to this theme.

He Comes Quickly - Onearth Gathering. Maui, Hawaii.
1981

The Messiah is likened unto an orgasm;

When he comes,

He comes quickly.*

* Matthew 25:1-13

The Story Wasn't Exciting Enough – 1982

Letter to President Barack Obama

President of the United States   November 6, 2015
Barack Obama
1600 Pennsylvania Ave. N.W.
Washington D.C. 20500

Re: Associated Press article in Maui News: **Obama Calls For Chance For Inmates After Prison**

Dear President Obama,

In **1979** you left **Hawaii** for **Chicago** and in **1979** my wife and I arrived in Maui, **Hawaii** from **Chicago.** My brother is Dr. **Craig** R. Travis M.D. My wife and I were both born at the Lying in Hospital in **Hyde Park.** I am from the **S.W. side** of Chicago. We are both Democrats. We met your half sister **Maya** at our Jewish Synagogue in 2008. I am 67 years old, an ex-felon, and I have been served a terrible injustice in Hawaii. I need your help.

On **January 20, 2009**, the day of your inauguration, I self surrendered to the Federal Detention Center in Honolulu, Hawaii for tax offenses not related to evasion or fraud. Up to that time I was a successful real estate agent in Hawaii since 1979 having obtained my broker's license in 1982 and opening up my own company. I became a licensed agent in Chicago in 1969 and a broker in 1971. I served 21 months of a 24 month sentence. While I was in prison the DCCA filed a motion for summary judgment to revoke my real estate broker's license due to the prior conviction. I had a hearing in September 2010, was released in October 2010 and in December 2010 the hearings officer who is the Chief Justice for the Intermediate Court of Appeals recommended to the Real Estate Commission that my license be revoked because I was an ex felon.

The attorney I hired did the best he could for the $25.00 per hour he charged me and I got what I paid for. He did not do enough research to discover that Hawaii has three specific mandatory statutes that prevent revocation of a professional or vocational license unless the crime/offense is directly related to the profession or vocation. The state of Hawaii in their case against me never once established any relationship between my duties as a real estate broker and my tax offenses. They also admitted no consumer complaints against me in my entire career. The State in their Findings of Fact and Conclusions of Law admitted in writing that the recommended revocation was based on prior conviction, but later in court denied it. On April 29, 2011 my license was revoked for 5 years. Since that time life has been an extreme hardship without the income from my profession I worked so hard for 42 years. Our marriage of 40 years is all but over. Our home of 25 years is in foreclosure and my health has suffered due to the enormous stress I am under.

Immediately after the revocation we filed an appeal to the First Circuit Court of Hawaii and was denied. We then filed an appeal to the Intermediate Court of Appeals (ICA) and I was denied. (The hearing's officer in my case is the Chief Justice for the ICA.) My attorney became too ill to practice law and so, due to lack of finances, I filed a Writ of Mandamus Pro Se to the State Supreme Court and was denied. I proved incontrovertibly in my Writ my grounds for Mandamus yet the State Supreme Court in their denial stated: "...it appears that petitioner fails to demonstrate that he has a clear and indisputable right to extraordinary relief or that he lacked alternative means to seek relief..." The Writ proves otherwise. Had the State of Hawaii invoked *HRS 831; HRS 831-3.1 (a-d); HRS Section 378-2(1) and 378-2.5(a)* which all state in relevant parts: "A person shall not be disqualified from...employment...**by the state** <u>or</u> **any...of its agencies**...or be disqualified to pursue...any profession...for which a license..is required **solely by reason of a prior conviction of a crime**......unless a person has been convicted of a crime that bears a rational relationship to the duties and responsibilities of a job...For the purpose of this subsection, such refusal..**revocation may occur** <u>only</u> when the agency determines, AFTER INVESTIGATION...that the **person so convicted has not been sufficiently rehabilitated to warrant the public trust."** The state conducted no investigation into my rehabilitation.

The State agencies had no legal grounds to revoke my license. I was denied my due process rights by not being able to prove my 100% rehabilitation by the federal government to the State. Because the state hid the statutes that prevented revocation I lost my civil rights and as a result the real estate commission did not have subject matter jurisdiction to revoke my license.

I have enclosed my Writ of Mandamus and other exhibits which tells the whole legal story. The *Hawaii Civil Rights Commission* says they cannot help me; the *United States Equal Employment Opportunity Commission (EEOC)* cannot help me; the *ACLU* cannot help me; I even asked for leniency from the real estate commission but they said: "...it is highly inappropriate for the Commission, as well as any state employee, to insert themselves into a contested case **and attempt to disregard the rule of law as outlined in HRS**." It is the state who created this nightmare for me by "disregarding the rule of law as outlined in the HRS" to begin with. I cannot get justice in the state court system for obvious reasons.

My situation, like thousands of other ex-felons, is quite desperate both financially and emotionally. I have been discriminated against because of my status as an ex-felon. I have been treated like a third class citizen with a stigma attached. Hawaii was the first state to initiate the "ban the box" law yet the real estate license application still asks the question: "Have you been convicted of a crime in the past 20 years?" Ex-felons in Hawaii have no chance at getting their lives back. It is just the way it is. This is the truth. The state did everything to harm me when it was supposed to help me. Inmates have very little chance after prison. I am living proof. I went to Governor Abercrombie three times and was denied. I wrote to him to pardon my revocation to no avail.

Mr. President, Article II of the United States Constitution explicitly assigns to the President the executive power to grant reprieves and pardons. I ask that you please grant me a reprieve from this unjust revocation and restore my real estate broker's license to full active status. This would be a victory for all ex-felons in Hawaii and possibly the entire Union.

Sincerely,

Bruce Robert Travis
Kihei, Maui, Hawaii

Exhibits:

1) Article by the Associated Press as published in the Maui News November 3, 2015
2) Letter from the Real Estate Branch of the DCCA June 10, 2014
3) Writ of mandamus submitted on March 20, 2015
4) Order Denying Petition for a Peremptory Writ of Mandamus May 15, 2015
5) Response Letter from the Real Estate Branch of the DCCA to limit time of revocation July 23, 2015
6) Email to the United States Equal Employment Opportunity Commission (EEOC) July 30, 2015
7) Email response from the EEOC August 18, 2015
8) Letter from the Hawaii Civil Rights Commission September 8, 2015
9) Letter to the American Civil Liberties Union (ACLU) September 28, 2015
10) Letter from the ACLU October 5, 2015

EXHIBIT # 3

PETITION FOR PEREMPTORY WRIT OF MANDAMUS TO THE STATE SUPREME COURT OF THE STATE OF HAWAII

IN THE SUPREME COURT OF THE STATE OF HAWAII

TABLE OF CONTENTS

Writ of Mandamus or prohibition, but state that the petition may not exceed 30 pages, exclusive of disclosure statement, certificate of service and attachments. THIS WRIT OF MANDAMUS DOES NOT EXCEED 30 PAGES.

TABLE OF AUTHORITIES

CASES

STATUTES

OTHER

Page

DICTIONARY DEFINITIONS

EXHIBITS

IN THE SUPREME COURT OF THE STATE OF HAWAII

--- o O o ---

in re BRUCE ROBERT TRAVIS, Petitioner/Appellant, Pro Se

vs

DEPARTMENT OF COMMERCE & CONSUMER AFFAIRS (DCCA); REAL ESTATE COMMISSION (REC); REGULATED INDUSTRIES COMPLAINT OFFICE (RICO); CIRCUIT COURT OF THE FIRST CIRCUIT AND THE INTERMEDIATE COURT OF APPEALS (ICA), Respondents/Defendants-Appellees

NO. CAAP - 12 - 00000 46
CIVIL NO. 11-1-1090 (RAN)
REC 2008-228-L

PETITION FOR A PEREMPTORY WRIT OF MANDAMUS

March 20, 2015 I.

I. BACKGROUND

On July 26, 2007, Bruce Robert Travis, a Maui real estate broker, was indicted for obstructing and impeding the tax laws and for filing a false tax return. The tax years in question were 1996 to 2000. Travis plead guilty to one count of obstructing and impeding the tax laws, and one count to filing a false tax return. The following is a *Brief History of Time.*

July 26, 2007   - Travis indicted

117

April 2008   - Travis pleads guilty to two counts

December 2008   - Travis sentenced to 24 months in federal prison.

January 20, 2009 - Travis self-surrenders to the Federal Detention Center in Honolulu, Hawaii.

September 9, 2009 - RICO files petition for disciplinary action/motion for summary judgment pursuant to *HRS Chapters 91, 92* and *467.* The Real Estate Commission stated: "The Commission has jurisdiction pursuant to *HRS Sections 26-9, 92-17, 467-4 and 467-14.* [Exhibit 1]

March 10, 2010- Notice of Hearing and Pre-Hearing Conference-[Exhibit 2]

September 2010 - Hearing before the DCCA in Honolulu, Hawaii. *HRS Section 831-3.1 (a-d)* and *HRS Sections 378-2 & 378-2.5* not invoked by the DCCA to establish subject matter jurisdiction. Rehabilitation and establishing a rational relationship between Travis' tax offenses and his duties as a real estate broker according to the DCCA "not an issue..."

October 14, 2010 - Travis released from the Federal half way house.

December 28, 2010- Hearings officer (HO) Craig Uyehara recommends revocation based on Travis' prior conviction (HORO).

January 2011   - HO Amends recommended order.

April 29, 2011   - Real Estate Commission (REC) revokes Travis' license based on HO's recommended order (HORO).

August 1, 2011   - Travis files appeal to 1st Circuit Court *Civil No: 11-1-1090-05* (Agency appeal) DCCA *No. Rec 2008-228-L*

January 19, 2012 Order Denying Respondent/Appellant's Motion to Reconsider Order Affirming Commission's Final Order Filed 12/1/11. [Exhibit 3]

July 23, 2012   - Travis appeals to the Intermediate Court of Appeals (ICA).

September 10, 2012 - Merit panel assigned by the ICA.

December 17, 2014- Summary Disposition Order-Appeal to the ICA denied. [Exhibit 4]

II. Standard for Disposition

A writ of mandamus is an extraordinary remedy as a court order to government agency or another court to correct its previous illegal behavior in order to comply with the law. This mandamus should be issued to correct defects of justice. If a court judgment or action is a mistake it could seriously undermine the legitimacy of the entire legal process. Such writs are not meant to super cede the legal discretionary authority of the lower court, nor are they meant to serve as legal remedies in lieu of normal appellate procedures. Where the lower court has discretion to act, mandamus will not lie to control the exercise of that discretion, even when the court has acted erroneously, <u>unless</u> the Judge (s) has (1) <u>Exceeded his or her jurisdiction, (2) Has committed a flagrant and manifest abuse of discretion, or (3) has refused to act on a matter that is properly before the court under circumstances in which it has a legal duty to act. (Emphasis added).</u>

Petitioner/Travis will demonstrate to this high Supreme Court that the aforementioned agencies and courts:

1) Exceeded their jurisdiction.

2) Committed flagrant and manifest abuses of discretion by the failure to take into proper consideration the facts and law relating to *HRS Sections 831-3.1(a-d)* and *HRS Sections 378-2 and 378-2.5;* by committing an arbitrary and unreasonable departure from precedent, settled judicial custom, entirely against logic and the evidence, as an error of law and grounds for reversing the decision on appeal by the ICA.

3) Refused to act on a matter properly before the court that it had a legal duty to act.

At times, the government courts, departments or agencies (RICO, DCCA, REC) do not follow the articulated law. When a judicial authority can clearly show that **certain course of actions are mandated by law,** then the higher court can issue a writ of mandate. Likewise, a citizen can petition legal authority to issue a writ of mandate as a discretionary and equitable remedy which must be made in good faith.

A mandamus will only issue if: (1) There is **a demonstrated clear and indisputable right to the relief requested** and, (2) lack of other remedy. Petitioner appeals to this State Supreme Court to compel the hearing's officer Craig Uyehara, (HO) of the DCCA to perform his ministerial duties correctly and to uphold and enforce the mandatory and specific statute of *Hawaii Revised Statutes (HRS) Section 831-3. 1 (a-d)* which states in relevant part: "A person shall not be disqualified from..employment...by the state or any..of its agencies..or be disqualified to pursue..any profession..for which a license..is required **solely by reason of a prior conviction of a crime**..unless a person has been convicted of a crime **that bears a rational relationship to the duties and responsibilities of a job..**" *HRS Section 378-2.5. (Supp.2007)* states in relevant part: "...an employer may inquire about and consider an individual's **criminal conviction record**..concerning employment... **provided that the conviction bears a rational relationship to the duties and responsibilities of the position."**

The official ministerial duty of (HO) Craig Uyehara has no room for the exercise of discretion and the performance being required by the direct and positive command of the law. "It is elementary that the meaning of a statute must, in the first instance, be sought in the language in which the act is framed, and if that is plain, and if the law is within the constitutional authority of the law-making body which passed it, the sole function of the court is to enforce it according to its terms." *Lake County v Rollins, 130 U.S. 662,670,671; Bate Refrigerating Co. v. Sulzberger, 157 U.S. 1, 33; United States v Lexington Mill and Elevator Co., 232 U.S. 399,409; United States vBank, 234 U.S. 245,258; Carminetti v. U.S., 242 U.S. 470,485,489-493 (1916).*

"Our foremost obligation in construing a statute is to 'give effect to the intention of the legislature, which is to be obtained primarily from the language contained in the statute itself.'" *Hanabusa v. Lingle, 119 Hawaii 341,349,198 P.3d 604,612 (2008)*(internal quotations and citations omitted). "In so doing, we are bound to give effect to all parts of a statute, "no clause or sentence, or word shall be construed as superfluous, void, or insignificant. *State v Kaakimaka, 84 Hawai'i 280, 289-90, 933 P2d 617, 626-27(1997).*

The character of a duty as ministerial is to be determined by the nature of the act to be performed, and not by the office of the performer. Official duty is ministerial when it is absolute, certain and imperative, involving merely execution of a specific duty arising from fixed and designated facts; that a necessity may exist for the ascertainment of those facts does not operate to convert the act into one discretionary in its nature. *"State Ex REL School District v Ellis, 163 Neb 86 (NEB 19560.*

III. Statement of Jurisdiction

Petitioner Travis submits this Statement of Jurisdiction pursuant to the provisions of *HRAP rule 21(a)(i)(ii).* Pursuant to *HRS section 641-1,* petitioner Travis has statutory right to appeal to the Hawaii Supreme Court. *Rules 3 and 4* of the HRAP specify how a notice of appeal is taken and when a notice of appeal should be taken. Pursuant to *HRS Section 602-5 (1)* this court has jurisdiction to entertain this appeal. *HRS Section 602-5(3)* grants the Hawaii supreme court jurisdiction over writs of mandamus.

A lack of jurisdiction over subject matter cannot be waived, so the question of jurisdiction is in order at any stage of the case. Yamane v Pohlson, 111 HAW 74, 137, p 3 d 980, (Haw, 2006). Further, whenever there is a conflict between general and specific statutes regarding the same subject matter, the specific is favored. (Emphasis added) *Spirent Holding Corporation v. State Department of Taxation,* 121 HAW, 220, 228, 216, P3d 1243, 1251 (HAWapp 2009). The DCCA cited four general statutes in its petition as the basis for invoking subject matter jurisdiction to revoke Travis' real estate broker's license. "Although [a party] failed to raise its jurisdiction argument before the court in its appeal...,[i]t is well established...that lack of subject matter jurisdiction can NEVER (emphasis added) be waived by any party at any time." Chun v Employee's Ret. Sys. 73 Haw 9,13,828 2d 260,263 (1992)

The DCCA did not cite the specific statute *HRS Section 831-3.1 (a-d)* which concerns state agency efforts to revoke a business licence due to a defendant's prior criminal conviction.

The DCCA also did not cite to *Hawaii Revised Statutes (HRS) Section 378-2.5* - "Employer inquiries into conviction record history or credit report." The REC/DCCA/RICO did not have subject matter jurisdiction over the revocation of Travis' real estate broker's license. *HRS section 831-3.1(a-d)* deprives the aforementioned agencies jurisdiction. HRS Section 91-14(g) (2) which states in relevant part that a court may reverse the REC's final order if it was issued in excess of the statutory or jurisdiction of the agency.

The State of Hawaii has a strong commitment to the protection of civil rights. The legislature gave meaning to this commitment by creating the *Hawaii Civil Rights Commission (HCRC)* through enactment of *act 219* in 1988 and acts *386 and 387* in 1989. HCRC has enforced state laws prohibiting discrimination in employment. *HRS chapter 378, part I.*

In the **Hawai'i Supreme Court** ruling in the *ZakK. Shimose v Hawai'i Health Systems Corporation dba Hilo Medical Center No. SCWC-12-0000422* decided on **January 16, 2015** Recktenwald, C.J,Nakayama, McKenna, and Pollack, JJ, and Circuit Judge Alm, in place of Acoba, J., recused:

OPINION OF THE COURT BY NAKAYAMA, J.

"Subject to some restrictions, *Hawaii Revised Statutes (HRS) section 378-2.5* allows employers to deny employment based on an individual's conviction record **"provided that the conviction record bears a rational relationship to the duties and responsibilities of the position."** (emphasis added throughout). In 2007, Petitioner Zak K. Shimose(Shimose) applied for employment as a radiological technician (radtech) at Hawai'i Health Systems Corporation(HHSC) dba Hilo Medical Center (HMC)(collectively HHSC/HMC). HHSC/HMC rejected Shimose's application based solely on his prior conviction for possession with intent to distribute crystal methamphetamine. <u>The primary issue in this case is whether, as a matter of law, HHSC/HMC established the existence of a rational relationship between the radtech position and Shimose's prior drug conviction that would entitle it to summary judgment.</u> WE HOLD THAT IT DID NOT." (emphasis added).

The Shimose case is a near perfect parallel case to that of Appellant/Travis. The circumstances are nearly identical but with two very distinct differences. Shimose went to prison on drug charges and Travis went to prison on Tax offenses. The Defendants in the case of Shimose attempted to demonstrate a rational relationship between his drug conviction and being a radtech. The Hawai'i Supreme Court saw no such rational relationship.

In the case of Travis, the RICO/DCCA/REC established absolutely NO rational or logical relationship between his duties as a real estate broker and his tax related offences. No logical linkage of any kind was made at all. Yet, at the 10/12/11 circuit court hearing [TR: p.13 Exhibit 5] Attorney Kelly for the RICO/DCCA stated: "...the appellant cannot legitimately argue his conviction does not bear a rational relationship to the duties and responsibilities of a real estate license" WHERE IS THE RATIONAL RELATIONSHIP?

I. BACKGROUND: Shimose was convicted of possession with intent to distribute crystal methamphetamine on

August 28, 2001, and sentenced to 37 months in prison. While in prison, Shimose completed a bachelor's degree in philosophy at the University of Hawai'i, Hilo, and began investigating the radtech associates degree program at Kapiolani Community College (KCC). Shimose was released on March 7, 2003.

Shimose matriculated into KCC's radtech program in August of 2005. As part of the program, Shimose was assigned to HMC to complete a clinical rotation at HMC's imaging department. Shortly after the rotation began, HHSC/HMC concluded that Shimose's felony drug conviction **disqualified him** from participating in a clinical rotation at an HHSC facility, and removed him from the program. Shimose completed his clinical requirements at another medical facility and graduated from the radtech program in the spring of 2007.

Shimose applied for a vacant radtech position at HMC on June 15, 2007, and submitted a second application on July 30, 2007. In August of 2007, HMC verbally indicated that Shimose would not be hired for the radtech position. Shimose submitted a request for administrative review with HHSC/HMC on November 1, 2007. On September 16, 2008, HHSC/HMC sent Shimose a letter indicating that he was disqualified from consideration for the radtech position because of his conviction for possession with intent to distribute a controlled substance.

Shimose filed a complaint with the *Hawai'i Civil Rights Commission* (Commission) on September 6, 2008, alleging a violation of *HRS Section 378-2 (Supp.2007)* (*[1] "HRS *sec 378-2(Supp 2007)* provided then as it does now, in relevant part: (a) It shall be an unlawful discriminatory practice: (1)

Because of...**arrest and court record**...(A) For any employer to refuse to hire or employ or to bar or discharge from employment, or otherwise **to discriminate against any individual** in compensation or in the terms, conditions, or privileges of employment.") (Emphasis added throughout).

The Commission determined that the "medical center was lawfully entitled to consider {Shimose's} 2001 felony drug conviction in accordance with *HRS sec 378-2.5(1),* and the conviction disqualified [him] from the position." (*[2] "HRS 378-2.5(Supp. 2007) provided then as it does now, in relevant part: (a) Subject to subsection (b), an employer may inquire about and consider an individual's criminal conviction record concerning hiring, termination, or the terms, conditions, or privileges of employment; **provided that the conviction record bears a rational relationship to the duties and responsibilities of the position.**")

The Commission issued a notice of dismissal and right to sue letter on August 6, 2009. On October 25, 2009 Shimose filed suit in the circuit court alleging violations of *HRS sec 378-2* and *Article 1, Section 5 of the Hawai'i Constitution'"* (*[3] The Honorable Glenn S. Hara presided...") "Based on factual assertions made by HHSC/HMC it argued that it was entitled to summary judgment because a rational relationship existed between Shimose's conviction and the duties of a radtech...It argued that individuals with a felony drug conviction are **unfit** to handle controlled substances...**unfit** to handle non-controlled pharaceuticals...**unfit** to interact with patients..." et al.

Likewise, in Travis's case the DCCA citing the general statutes of *HRS sections 467-8, 436 B-19(a)(8)(12) and467-*

8(a)(3)'deemed Travis **"unfit..to hold a license"** and revoked the license of his real estate limited liability company prior to any recommended order(RO) by the Hearing's Officer (HO). The DCCA deemed Travis **"unfit"** because of his prior conviction and tax offences but established no rational linkage between the tax convictions and Travis' duties and responsibilities as a real estate broker.

"...Shimose disputed several of the material facts that HHSC/HMC had alleged...Based on the factual assertions (by Shimose) Shimose argued that the asserted relationship between the duties of a radtech and a felony drug conviction was irrationally based on biases and prejudices. Shimose argued that HHSC/HMC failed to establish that radtechs have access to controlled substances and that there was no rational relationship between a felony drug conviction and access to non-controlled substances or supplies...Shimose argued that issues of material fact surrounding HHSC/HMC's asserted rational relationships would preclude summary judgment in its favor."

As will be shown the revocation of Travis's real estate broker's license was "irrationally based on biases and prejudices" because of his tax offences and prior conviction with no rational relationship established by the DCCA in their case to the duties and responsibilities of being a real estate broker.

On March 28, 2012, the circuit court granted HHSC/HMC's motion for summary judgment and denied Shimose's cross-motion for summary judgment. The Intermediate Court of Appeals (ICA) affirmed.

II. STANDARD OF REVIEW in the Shimose State
Supreme Court case.

We review a circuit court's decision to grant a motion for summary judgment de novo under the standard that the circuit court should have applied. *Fujimoto v Au. 95 Hawai'i 116,136,19 P3d 699,719,(2001)* (citation omitted). "Summary judgment is appropriate if the pleadings, depositions, answers to interrogatories, and admissions on file, together with the affidavits, if any, show that there is no genuine issue of material fact and the moving party is entitled to judgment as a matter of law." *U.S. Bank Nat'l Ass'n v Castro, 131 Hawai'i 28,41,313 P3d 717, 730 (2013)*(internal quotations and citations omitted). **The evidence must be viewed in the light most favorable to the party opposing summary judgment.** See *Ralston v Yim. 129 Hawai'i 46,55-56,292 P3d 1276,1285-86 (2013)*.

In the Travis case, the HO wrongly concluded, pursuant to *HRS section 467-14(20)* that Appellant/Travis failed to maintain a record of honesty and truthfulness. However, there were insufficient facts and case law for this conclusion. Appellant submitted eleven "to whom it may concern" letters(which also constitute his record) showing that he had practiced as a real estate broker for nearly four decades and had a sterling reputation for honesty and truthfulness. According to *State ex rel. Bronster v Yoshina, 84 Haw. 179, 932, P 2d 316 (1997),* **the HO was legally required to view this evidence in the light most favorable to Travis.** However, the HO failed to follow *Yoshina* and relegated consideration of Appellant/Travis' letters only to the issue of sanctions. A review of the record shows that **the HO never considered any evidence in**

Travis' favor. The HO also wrongly concluded pursuant to *HRS sec 467-14(8) that* Appellant/Travis' conduct constituted fraudulent or dishonest dealing. Again, there were insufficient facts as well as case law upon which to draw this conclusion.

III DISCUSSION/Shimose: Several guidelines define the statutory phrase " rational relationship to the duties and responsibilities of the position, "HRS *sec 378-2.5(a)* which we previously interpreted in *Wright v Home Depot U.S.A., Inc., 111 Hawai'i 401,142 P3d 265 (2006)*. As stated in *Wright,* the rational relationship standard is not coextensive with the ultra-deferential rational basis test that is used in some equal protection cases. See *Wright, 111 Hawai'i at 412 n.9, 142 P 3d at 276 n.9.* Accordingly, **we decline to_adopt a standard under which virtually any conceivable state of facts could support an adverse employment decision.** (emphasis added throughout). Rather, **"the standard of rationality...**must find some footing in the realities of the subject." *Heller v Doe, 509 U.S. 312,321 (1993)*. As such, **an adverse employment action cannot be justified by an asserted relationship that is so remote or "attenuated as to render the distinction arbitrary or irrational."** *Fitzgerald v Racing Ass'n of Cent. Iowa, 539 U.S 103,106, (2003)(internal* quotations and citation omitted). **Negative attitudes toward politically unpopular ex-offenders do not, standing alone, justify adverse employment decisions;** Cf. *City of Cleburne v Cleburne Living Center, Inc.,* 473 U.S. 432, 446-47 (1985) (stating that **a base desire to harm a politically unpopular group is not a legitimate state interest);** *U.S. Department of Agriculture v Moreno, 413 U.S. 528 (1973).*(same). (* [8] See also *Elena Saxonhouse, Unequal Protection: comparing Former Felons'*

Challenges to Disenfranchisement and Employment Discrimination, 56 Stan Law Review 1597(2004).

B. LEGISLATIVE HISTORY OF HRS Section 378-2.5. These guidelines are supported by the legislative history of *HRS Sections 378-2 and 378-2.5,* which reveals that the statutory scheme was tailored to balance competing state interests. See *Life of the Land Inc., v City and County of Honolulu, 61 Haw. 390,447,606 P 2d 866, 899 (1980).* ("Courts may take legislative history into consideration in construing a statute.") Here, the legislative history of HRS section 378-2.5 reveals that **the legislature chose language broad enough to allow reasonable consideration of a record of conviction, but narrow enough to place a meaningful restraint on unlawful discrimination.** See *S. Stand. Comm. Rep. No. 3282, in 1998 Senate Journal at 1331* ("The intent of this bill is to provide a balanced disclosure taking into account the interest of the employee and the employer.")

Since the majority of real estate agents and brokers are independent contractors and not employees, the RICO/DCCA/REC acts as a clearing house so to speak, a pseudo employer for all real estate agents and brokers that determines who becomes licensed(gainfully employed) or not. In the broader view the DCCA/REC is the master employer and is bound by statute the same as any employer of any business.

"The fundamental restraint on discrimination against persons with conviction records embodied in HRS section 378-2 was passed into law in 1974 to reflect the legislature's recognition "that **persons who have been in trouble are not inherently and permanently bad** and that opportunities afforded other citizens should be made available to them." *S.Stand. Comm. Rep No. 862-74, in 1974 Senate Journal at 1079.* The purpose of *HRS section 378-2 "is* **to encourage the** <u>rehabilitation</u> **of convicted persons by eliminating disqualification from employment...solely by reason of a prior conviction of a crime."** Id. (emphasis in original)(emphasis added by Travis). **Convicted persons who are rehabilitated** through meaningful employment show decreased levels of recidivism. (*9 See, e.g. <u>Matthew Makarios</u> et al., Examining the Predictors of Recidivism among men and women released from prison in Ohio, 37 Crim. Just. & Behav. 1377(2010).)

Shimose continued: "In 1998, a bill introduced in the House proposed a dramatic policy reversal by deleting the phrase "court record" from HRS section 378-2. This would have allowed employers to consider criminal convictions without restraint. The House Standing Committee Report accompanying the bill stated: The purpose of this bill is to **repeal the prohibition against employment discrimination based upon arrest and court record.**...Your Committee finds that under current law, **it is an unlawful discriminatory practice in connection with employment to discriminate on the basis of an individual's arrest and court record.** Your Committee believes that the **rehabilitation** of individuals who may have run afoul of the law is **essential to society** and that **gainful employment is necessary to the rehabilitative process.** Your Committee is concerned, however, that broad prohibitions restricting an employer's right to question a person regarding criminal convictions may compromise the safety of customers and employees.

Upon careful consideration, your Committee has amended this measure by:

(3)   Limiting the prohibition against unlawful discriminatory practices in employment because of "arrest and court record" under *Section 378-2(1), HRS,* to "arrest records";

(4)   Adding a new definition of "Arrest record" to *Section 378-1, HRS,* which definition **excludes records of criminal conviction,** thereby effectively **providing an exception to the prohibition against unlawful discriminatory practices in employment on the basis of an applicant's or current employee's record of criminal conviction [.]"**

H. Stand. Comm. Rep. No. 673-98, in 1998 House Journal at 1300-01. The House's proposal was opposed by the Senate Standing Committee, which issued a report that stated:

Your Committee is concerned that this measure will diminish the employment opportunities for individuals who have a conviction record. Your Committee believes that it is in our State's best interest to see to it that these individuals not be discriminated against in their search for employment should these individuals be unable to secure employment. Should these individuals be unable to secure employment and turn to public assistance or return to a life of crime, the costs will be borne by the public.

Your Committee has amended this bill by:

(2) Inserting a provision to allow employers to inquire about conviction records, provided that it is done so only after the employer makes a conditional offer of employment and that

the conviction record bears a rational relationship to the employment duties of the position that has been offered; (emphasis added throughout.)

(3) Inserting a provision that limits the inquiry to the past five years;
(4) Inserting a requirement that the employer shall make an individualized assessment of the circumstances associated with the record of conviction and any **evidence of rehabilitation** to determine if the person is suitable for employment[.] *S.Stand. Comm. Rep. No.2959, in 1998 Senate Journal at 1207-08.*" The DCCA considered no evidence and made no "individualized assessment" in Travis' case.

"Negotiations came down to the final day, and "agreement on th[e] measure was reached approximately one hour before the deadline." The resulting compromise, enacted as HRS Section 378-2.5, **allows consideration of a criminal conviction that bears a "rational relationship to the duties and responsibilities of the position."** The Statutory language adopted did not embody the House's proposal to allow unfettered consideration of criminal convictions. The legislature also rejected the Senate's proposal for a "substantial relationship" standard. (*10 *HRS Section 378-2.5* also adopted the Senate's provision that requires employers to make a conditional job offer before inquiring into conviction history, but rejected the Senate's proposal that would have required employers to make an individualized assessment of the circumstances associated with an applicants conviction history. An overly broad reading of *HRS Section 378-2.5* would eviscerate the **protections afforded to persons with conviction records** by *HRS Sections 378-2 and 2.5.,* and render the statutory phrase "duties and responsibilities" meaningless. That was not the bicameral intent of the enacting legislature."

HCRC Section 378-2- discriminatory practices made unlawful; offences defined. It shall be an unlawful discriminatory practice:

1) Because of race, sex, including gender identity or expression, sexual orientation, age, religion, color, ancestry, disability, marital status, **arrest and court record** (emphasis added throughout).
(B) For any employment agency to fail or refuse to refer for employment or to classify or to otherwise to discriminate against any individual.
2) For any employer, labor organization or employment agency to discharge, expel, or otherwise discriminate against any individual because the individual has opposed any practice forbidden by this or has filed a complaint, testified or assisted in any proceeding respecting the discriminatory practices prohibited under this part.

HCRC Section 378-2. 5(a)- employer **inquiries into conviction record.**

(a) Subject to subsection (b) an employer may inquire about and consider an individual's criminal conviction record concerning hiring, termination, or the terms, conditions or privileges of employment; **provided that the conviction record bears a rational relationship to the duties and responsibilities of the position.** (see *HRS section 831-3.1, (c) (2)*

(c) For purposes of this section "<u>conviction</u>" means an adjudication by a court of competent jurisdiction that the defendant committed a crime, not including final judgements required to be confidential pursuant to *HCRC section 571-84;* provided that the employer may consider the employee's conviction record falling within a period that shall not exceed the most recent 10 years.

HCRC Section 378-4- Enforcement Jurisdiction- the *Hawaii Civil Rights Commission* **shall have jurisdiction over the subject of discriminatory practices made unlawful by this part.** Travis' statute of limitations ran out 90 days after his licensed was revoked on 4/29/11.

The *United States Equal Employment Opportunity Commission* (EEOC) compliance manual advises that employers cannot enact a "<u>blanket exclusion of persons convicted of any crime.</u>" Employers can reject an applicant with a criminal conviction <u>if the employer can demonstrate that the reason was job related</u>. In 2012 the EEOC issued guidelines that list removing the <u>criminal background</u> test practices in the hiring process. The EEOC guidelines also say employers should <u>be able to show a nexus between any hiring restriction placed on felons</u> and the jobs they are applying for, for **not doing so could open up the employer to civil rights litigation.**

The *EEOC* has interpreted the *Civil Rights Act* to require that, where an **employment policy of a state,** municipal or private employer that discriminates against criminals will have a disparate racial impact **employers must show a business necessity before automatically, disqualifying criminals.** California law, e.g. provides that <u>a criminal record can</u>

affect ones application for a professional license **only** if **"the crime or act is substantially related to the_ qualifications, functions and duties of the business or profession** for which the application is made. *HRS Section 831-3.1 (a-d)* requires the same thing. Because Travis was an ex felon he was discriminated against. There was no legal basis for "disqualifying" Travis for his real estate broker's license because of his prior conviction. This was a violation of his most basic civil rights. He was in prison for twenty one months and when he was released the RICO/DCCA put Travis in unemployment prison. The HHSC/HMC tried to do the same thing to Shimose and even the *Hawaii Civil Rights Commission* dismissed Shimose's claim and right to sue but Shimose knew the law and filed suit in the circuit court alleging statutory violations. Is Travis' case any different in principle? The "employment policy" of the DCCA/RICO/REC was to "discriminate against criminals" and to "disqualify criminals" from employment.

IV. Discussion-Travis Case

The sole issue in the Travis proceeding is whether the RICO, DCCA and REC exceeded the bounds of their authority, committed a flagrant and manifest abuse of discretion, committed unlawful acts and reversible errors, committed illegal behavior, exceeded their jurisdiction and refused to act on a matter properly before the court under circumstances in which it had a legal duty to act. "A writ of Mandamus...will not issue unless the petitioner demonstrates a clear and indisputable right to relief and a lack of alternative means to redress the alleged wrong or obtain the requested action." State v Hamili, 87 Hawaii 102, 104, 952 p 2d 39 d, 392 (1998); citing Straub

Clinic & Hospital v Kochi, 81 Hawaii 410, 414, 917, p 2d 1284, 1288; to follow the articulated law when their course of actions were mandatory and specific to statutes *HRS section 831-3.1 (a-d) and HRS 378-2 and 378-2.5.*

HRS section 831-3: Rights <u>Retained by convicted person</u>. (Emphasis added throughout) "Except as otherwise provided by law, **a person convicted of a crime does not suffer civil death** or corruption of blood **or sustain loss of civil rights** or forfeiture of estate or property, but **retains all the person's rights, political, personal, civil,** and otherwise, including **the right to** hold public office or **employment,** to vote, to hold, receive and transfer property, to enter into contracts, to sue and be sued, and to hold offices of private trust in accordance of law "{ 1 1969, c 250, PT of sec. 1; HRS sec 716-3; RENL 1972, c9, pt of section 1; gen ch 1985, am L 1986, c 155 section 2; am L 2003, c 95, sec 16 (1) }

HRS section 831-3. 1 (a-d) 'Uniform act on status of convicted persons. **A person shall not be disqualified from** public office or **employment <u>BY THE STATE</u>** or any of its branches, political_subdivisions **<u>OR AGENCIES</u>** except under section *831-2 (c);* **or be disqualified** to practice, pursue, or engage in any occupation, trade, vocation profession, or business for which a permit, license, registration, or certificate is required by the state or any of its branches, political subdivisions, or agencies, **solely by reason of a prior conviction of a crime,** provided that (2) a person who within ten years, excluding any period of incarceration has been convicted of a crime that **<u>bears a rational relationship to the duties and responsibilities of a job,</u>** occupation, trade, vocation, profession, or business may be denied employment a permit, license, registration or certificate, nothing in this subsection shall abrogate any applicable appeal rights under chapters 76 or 89.

(b)   The state or any of its branches, political subdivisions or agencies may consider as a justification for the refusal, suspension, or license, registration or certificate, any conviction of any crime, except those which have been expunged occurring within the past ten years, excluding any period of incarceration, **when that crime bears a rational relationship to the duties and responsibilities of the job,** occupation trade, vocation, profession or business for which a permit, license, registration or certificate is applied for or held.

(b)   **The state** or any of its branches, political subdivisions, **or agencies** may consider as a possible justification for the refusal, suspension, or **revocation of** any employment or of **any** permit **license,** registration, or certificate, any conviction of a crime, not occurring within the past ten years, excluding any period of incarceration, except those which have been expunged, when the offense directly relates to:

(1) The applicant's possible performance in the job applied for.

(2) The employee's possible performance in the job that the employee holds; or.

(3) The applicant's or holder's possible performance in the occupation, trade, vocation, profession, or business for which a permit, license, registration, or certificate is applied for or held.

For the purpose of this subsection, **such** refusal, suspension or **revocation may occur only** when the agency determines, **AFTER INVESTIGATION** (Emphasis added throughout) in accordance with chapter 91, or in the case of employment in the civil service, after appropriate, investigation, notification of results and planned action, and opportunity to meet and rebut the finding, all of which need not be conducted in accordance with chapter 91; **that the person so convicted has not been sufficiently rehabilitated to warrant the public trust.**

(d) When considering non criminal standards in the granting, renewal, suspension, or revocation of any employment or any such permit, license, registration, or certificate, the state or any of its branches, political subdivisions or agencies **shall not take into consideration the conviction of any crime** except as provided by subsections ' (b) and (c)."

The DCCA hearing's officer (HO) Craig Uyehara, a judge with the Intermediate Court of Appeals (ICA) allowed the appellee/DCCA to proceed with its case against Travis without satisfying the elements of *HRS section 831-3.1 (a-d) and HRS Sections 378-2 and 378-2.5;* i.e. that Travis had been "convicted of crimes that bore a **rational** relationship to the duties and responsibilities" of being a real estate broker. The word "rational" according to Webster means "manifesting or based upon reason; "i.e. logical." Filing a false tax return or obstructing the tax laws(filing arbitration and litigation against the IRS) have no logical relationship to the duties and responsibilities of being a real estate broker. The complete record shows the RICO, DCCA and REC **NEVER** presented **ANY** evidence in their case to establish such a "logical" linkage. The REC did not have subject matter jurisdiction to adjudicate

Travis' case because the RICO, DCCA and REC **NEVER** established that the requirements of *HRS section 831-3. 1 (a-d)* and *HRS Sections 378-2 and 378-2.5* were met. As a result the HO committed reversible errors.

The RICO, DCCA and REC **NEVER** demonstrated that Travis tax offense was "job related." **NOT ONCE.** The DCCA's position is that *HRS section 831-3.1 (a-d)* "is not an issue in this matter." See transcript 10/12/11 page 14[Exhibit 6] The DCCA argues that *HRS section 831-3. 1 (a-d)* does not apply in this case because the commission REC/ DCCA/ RICO, did not discipline Travis based on his conviction. [Exhibit 6]The record, however belies this false claim.

The DCCA submitted Exhibit # 2 which was Travis' Federal **criminal conviction record.** In fact and in truth, **the HO** himself **admitted that he recommended the discipline of revoking** Travis' real estate broker's **license** (subsequently adopted in whole by the REC) **based on** Travis' **criminal conviction** when HO Craig Ueyhara stated that Travis allegedly violated *HRS Section 467-14 (20)* as follows:

"Respondent's **criminal conviction is OF RECORD and that conviction constitutes** a failure to maintain a record of honesty and truthfulness." [Exhibit 7 p. 14]. But, *HRS Section 378-2* states: "It shall be an **unlawful discriminatory practice** for any employer to refuse to hire or employ...any individual...because of...arrest and **COURT RECORD."** State agencies are not exempt from the violation of this statute. It is an "unlawful discriminatory practice." The plain language of *HRS 831-3.1 (a-d)* is manifestly clear. "A person shall not be disqualified from...employment **by the state or**

any of its...agencies...solely by reason of a prior conviction of a crime..."

"When construing a statute the court's foremost obligation is to ascertain and give effect to the intention of the legislature which is to be obtained primarily from the language contained in the statute itself." Id *City and County of Honolulu v Ing., 100 Hawaii 182,189,58 P3d 1229,1236(2002); State vs Kamal, 88 Hawaii 292, 294,966 P2d 604,606(1998);* "where the statutory language is unambiguous, the court's sole duty is to give effect to its plain and obvious meaning." Id *State v Harada, 98 Hawai'i 18,41,41 P3d 174,197(2002); State v Kalama, 94 Hawai'i 60,64, 8P 3d 1224,1228(2000).* Regulation cannot deviate from statute or it is void. The **state agencies are bound by statute.** (emphasis added). "What does not exist in regulation or statute does not exist at all. *"Carminetti v. U.S., 242 U.S. 470,485, 489-493 (1916).* Legislation and its intent, on state and federal levels, is the governing factor in determining unlawfulness or legality, and that no agency or court has the authority to deviate from it or expand its application to subjects not expressly implicated or addressed."

It is *HRS Section 831-3.1 (a-d)* and *HRS Sections 378-2* and *378-2.5* which provides the prescription for deciding Travis' challenges to the RICO, DCCA and REC all of which are founded squarely upon the strict interpretation of the statutory language to show those state agencies the lack of statutory authority they give to the four general statutes they cited to revoke Travis' license. What this case has evoked from the RICO, DCCA and REC is a challenge to Travis' strict interpretation of the statute with the DCCA/RICO/REC denying the Statute's relevance. In such an instance as the latter, a particular approach to the controversy must be taken.

"The parties provide vastly differing interpretations of the statutory language, and both contend that the language clearly supports their position." The State agencies revoked Travis's license based on four GENERAL statutes and their language and thus supported by the Circuit and Intermediate Courts as if the SPECIFIC and mandatory statute of *HRS 831-3.1(a-d)* (and *HRS 378-2 & 378-2.5)* played no part in the case at all. The construing court's duty is "to find that interpretation which can most fairly be said to be imbedded in the statute, in the sense of being most harmonious with its scheme and with the general purposes that Congress manifested. The circumstances of the enactment of particular legislation may be particularly relevant to this inquiry. Finally, when there is reasonable doubt about the meaning of a revenue statute, for example, **the doubt is resolved in favor of those taxed.** As in all cases of statutory interpretation, we must start with the text of the statute..." *Security Bank of Minnesota v. Commissioner of IRS,* 994, F 2d 432,435-36 (CA8 1993). "In construing a statute, it is safer always not to add to, or subtract from, the language of the statute unless imperatively required to make it...rationale..." *State v Taylor,* 97 Wn. 2D 724,728,649 P. 2d 633 (1982). "A well established general rule is that where a statute expressly provides for stated exceptions, no other exceptions will be implied." Insurance Co. of N.Am.Co. V Sullivan, 56, Wn 2d 251, 352, P 2d 193 (1960). *"The office of a proviso generally is either to except something from the enacting clause, or to qualify or to restrain its generality, or to exclude some possible ground of misinterpretation of it, as extending to cases not intended by the legislature to be brought* within its purview...." (Wash) Attorney *General Opinion 65-66No. 69.*

The RICO, DCCA and REC discriminated against Travis and revoked his license based solely upon his prior conviction contravening the statutory laws. They did not even recognize *HRS 8313.1 (a-d)* as being relevant at all. If the RICO, DCCA, REC, Circuit Court and Intermediate Court of Appeals do not correct its defects of justice their illegal and unlawful actions could seriously undermine the legitimacy of the civil rights of all prior convicted felons. Those agencies and courts have a "legal duty to act," upon the plain unambiguous language of the specific mandatory statute of *HRS section 831-3. 1 (a-d)*, mandated by the *Hawaii Legislature,* the Hawaii *State Constitution (HSC) Article 1 Section 5*(raised by Shimose in his appeal) and the *Hawaii Civil Rights Commission Sections 378-1. 378-2 (1) (b) (2); 378-2. J (a) (b) (c) (d) (1) and 378-4.*

"No person shall be deprived of life, liberty or <u>property</u> without due process of law, nor be denied the enjoyment of the person's <u>civil rights,</u> or be discriminated against in the exercise thereof because of race, religion, sex or ancestry. "The *Hawaii State Constitution* is patterned after the 14th amendment of the *United States Constitution. HSC Article 1, Section 2.* "<u>Rights</u> of individuals. All persons are free by nature and are equal in their inherent and inalienable <u>rights,</u> among these <u>rights</u> are the enjoyment of life, liberty and the pursuit of happiness, and the acquiring and possessing of **property.** These <u>rights</u> cannot endure unless the people recognize their corresponding, obligations and responsibilities."

Amendment IV Section 1 USC. "All persons born or naturalized in the United States, and subject to the jurisdiction thereof, are citizens of the United States and of the state wherein they reside. **No state shall make or enforce any law which shall abridge the privileges or immunities of citizens of the United States;** nor shall any state deprive any person of life, liberty or **property,** without due process of law; nor deny to any person within its jurisdiction the equal protection of the laws." (emphasis added). The RICO, DCCA and REC did not offer Travis "the equal protection of the laws" and denied him "due process" by not invoking *HRS Section_ 831-3.1(a-d) and HRS 378-2 and 378-2.5.*

Article, 1 Section 8 Hawaii State Constitution -Rights of citizens - no citizen shall be disenfranchised or deprived of any of the rights or privileges secured to other citizens, unless by the law of the land." "No person shall be deprived of life, liberty or **property** without due process of law   **What   is "property"?**

In the United States Supreme Court ruling of <u>*Butcher's Union Co v Crescent City. Co*</u> 111 U.S. 746 (1884) Chief Justice Field, concurring, cited to Adam Smith's *Wealth of Nations,* Book I Ch 10. "It has been well said that the **property** (emphasis added throughout) which every man has is **his own labor,** as it is the original foundation of all other property so it is the most sacred and inviolable. The patrimony of the poor man lies in the strength and dexterity of his own hands, and to hinder his employing this strength and dexterity in what manner he thinks proper, without injury to his neighbor, is a plain violation of this most sacred property. It is manifest encroachment upon the just liberty both of the workman and of those who might be disposed to employ him. As it hinders the one from working at what he thinks proper, so it hinders the others from employing whom they think proper"

Labor is property

"Labor is the most sacred and inviolable of all property and the original foundation of all other property." The RICO, DCCA, REC, Circuit Court and Intermediate Court of Appeals denied Travis his most fundamental civil rights guaranteed to him by the *U.S. Constitution* and the *Hawaii State Constitution* which is superior to any general statute of the Hawaii revised statutes.

Adair v U.S. 208 US 161 (1908) - "In our opinion that section in the personal liberty as well as the right of **property,** guaranteed by the amendment,(14th) such liberty and right embrace the right to make contracts for the purchase of the labor of others, and equally the right to make contracts for the sale of one's own labor; (emphasis added throughout) each right, however, being subject to the fundamental condition that no contract whatever its subject-matter, can be sustained which the law, upon reasonable grounds, forbids as inconsistent with the public interests, or as hurtful to the public order, or as detrimental to the common good. The right to purchase or to sell labor is part of the liberty protected by this amendment unless there are circumstances which exclude the right ... in every case that comes before this court, therefore, where legislation of this character is concerned. And where the protection of the federal Constitution is sought; the question necessarily arises; is this a fair, reasonable, and appropriate exercise of the police power of the state, or is it an unreasonable, unnecessary and arbitrary interference with the right of the individual to his personal liberty, or to enter into those contracts in relation to labor which may seem to be inappropriate or necessary **for the support of himself and his family,** of course, the liberty of contract relating to labor includes both parties to it. The one has as much right to purchase as the other to sell labor.

Coopage v State of Kansas, 236 US 1 (1915). "The principle is fundamental and vital. Included in the right of private property and right of personal liberty, partaking of the nature of each- is the right to make contracts for the acquisition of property. Chief among such contracts is that of personal employment, by which labor and other services are exchanged for money or other forms of property. If this right be struck down or arbitrarily interfered with there is a substantial impairment of liberty in the long-established constitutional sense. The right is as essential to the laborer as to the capitalist, to the poor as to rich; for the vast majority of persons have no other honest way to begin to acquire property, save by working for money." The rights of personal liberty and private property are "fundamental and vital." The right to make contracts for the acquisition of property, chief among such contracts is that of personal employment."

Hearings officer, Craig Ueyhara, for the DCCA failed to perform his ministerial duty of the single act of upholding and enforcing *HRS section 831-3. 1 (a-d)*. Travis has a clear right to relief. *FR and S Inc v Commonwealth of Pennsylvania, Department of Environmental Resources, 104pa cm with, 647, 522 a 2d 1190 (1987);* A corresponding duty exists with defendants, RICO, DCCA, REC, the Circuit Court and the ICA. *Williams v Worley, 847 A 2 d 134 (PA CMWLTH 2004)*

HRS section 831-3. 1 (3) -**"...that (after Investigation) the person so convicted has not been sufficiently rehabilitated to warrant the public trust."** HO Craig Uyehara did not properly weigh the evidence of Travis' rehabilitation or conduct any investigation into his rehabilitation.

"Condemnation without investigation is the highest form of ignorance." Albert Einstein

"There is a principle which is a bar against all information, which is proof against all information, which is proof against all arguments and which cannot fail to keep a man in everlasting ignorance: that principle is **contempt prior to investigation"** Herbert Spencer.

"Search for evidence of truth with diligence and honesty, and be heartily ready to receive evidence whether for the agreement or disagreement of ideas. Search with diligence, spare no labor in searching for the truth in due proportion to the importance of the proposition. Search with a steady honesty of soul and sincere impartiality to find the truth. Do not indulge yourself to wish any unexamined proposition were true or false; a wish often perverts the judgment and tempts the mind strangely to believe upon slight evidence whatsoever we wish to be true or false. Isaac Watt. *Logic, Or the Right Use of Reason In The Inquiry After Truth.* Pp 230, 231.

"We human beings know so little, and understand so little less still, that it is just foolish to come to conclusions on the basis of what we think should or should not be, or by wishful thinking or prejudices or just what we want to believe. **Condemna-**

tion prior to investigation leads to error, not truth." Adam Rutherford *Pyramidology* Vol.1.

"He that answereth a matter before he heareth it, it is folly and shame unto him." - *Proverbs 18:13*

"Prove all things; hold fast that which is good." *Thessalonians 5:21*

"Great spirits have always encountered violent opposition from mediocre minds." Albert Einstein.

The RICO, DCCA and REC condemned Travis without any investigation. The ICA states on page 5 par 3 in their *Summary Disposition Order:* [Exhibit 4] "Here, Travis participated in the administrative hearing, presented evidence, and appealed the Commission's Final Order, arguing before the Circuit Court. Any argument that Travis did not receive sufficient notice of the charge based upon *HRS 467-14(20)* due to the erroneous citation to HRS 467-14(2) is without merit."

It is true Travis was given notice of a hearing before the DCCA in September 2010[Exhibit 2] but because the DCCA did not cite to the specific mandatory statute of *HRS Section 831-3.1(a-d)* or *HRS 378-2 and378-2.5* Travis was **not** given "sufficient notice" of the existence of these specific statutes that protected ex-felon's civil rights. As a result Travis was denied his *4th and 14th Amendment Constitutional Rights* to due process of law and as a result was denied the "equal protection of the laws" mandated in those amendments. Travis was given insufficient bogus notice and was literally defrauded out of his civil and constitutional rights suspending any statute of limitations for suit with any of the state and federal agencies. Secondly, all four of the general statutes cited by the DCCA to re-voke Travis' license are moot. *HRS Section 831-3.1(a-d)* su-per-cedes and is superior to those junior statutes when *Sec. 831* is at issue.

As to Travis' procedural due process rights the ICA on page 5[Exhibit 4] cites to *State vBani, 97 Hawai'i 285, 293,36P. 3d 1255, 1263 (2001)* stating: "...However, we have repeatedly recognized that due process is not a fixed concept requiring a specific procedural course in every situation. Instead, due process is flexible and calls for such procedural protections as the particular situation demands." Id at *296, 36P.3dat 1266.* This "particular situation" demanded the protection of Travis' Constitutional civil rights pursuant to the *HSC,* the *USC,* the *HCRC,* the *EEOC* and *HRS Sec. 831-3.1(a-d), 378-2, 378-2.5* and should allow for no flexibility whatsoever.

Black's Law Dictionary 6ᵗʰ Ed. p. 500 defines Due Process as follows: "Law in its regular course of administration through courts of justice. Due Process of law in each particular case means such an exercise of the powers of the government as the settled maxims of law permit and sanction, and under such safeguards for the protection of individual rights as those max-ims prescribe for the class of cases to which the one in ques-tion belongs. A course of legal proceedings according to those rules and principles which have been established in our sys-tems of jurisprudence **for the enforcement and protection of private rights.** To give such proceedings any validity, there must be a tribunal competent by its constitution-that is, by the law of its creation-to pass upon the subject matter of the suit...*Pennoyer vNeff, 95 U.S. 733, 24L. Ed 565...*Due process of law implies the right of the person affected thereby to be present before the tribunal which pronounces judgment upon the question of life, liberty, or property, in its most comprehensive sense; to be heard by testimony or otherwise, and have the right of **controverting, by proof, every material fact**(emphasis added) which bears on the question of right in the matter involved. If any question of fact or liability be conclusively presumed against him, **this is not due process of law."**

The presumption of rehabilitation in *HRS Sec. 831-3.1(a-d)* is exactly this **"material fact"** omitted deliberately by the DCCA/REC/RICO that Travis did not have an opportunity to provide the evidence of **his complete rehabilitation** and place the burden upon the state to rebut this presumption of Travis' complete rehabilitation. In this case Travis' due process IS a "fixed concept" allowing no flexibility in relation to his inalienable right to "life, liberty, property and the pursuit of happiness;" his most fundamental and sacred civil rights. Shimose p.5: "Convicted persons who are **rehabilitated** through meaningful employment show decreased levels of recidivism." "The purpose of *HRS Section 378-2* is to encourage the **rehabilitation of convicted persons by eliminating disqualification from employment...solely by reason of a prior conviction of a crime."** Why didn't the RICO, DCCA or REC know this? Why was Travis disqualified from employment because of his prior conviction?

The Hawaii attorney general *(AG) in Opinion Letter No. 61-26 citing to United States v Carrollo,* has taken the position that the state cannot revoke a real estate salesman's license on the basis of his conviction for a failure to file tax returns. The Hawaii attorney general in *Opinion Letter No 89* -1 has also suggested that **before the state can revoke a real estate li-**

cense, pursuant to *HRS section 831-3,1 (a-d)*, <u>it has to establish that the licensee had **NOT** been sufficiently rehabilitated.</u> Further, *Opinion Letter no 89-1* cites to <u>*Marra v City of White Plains*, 96 ad 2d 17 467 N.Y.S 2 D 865 (app av. 1983)</u> which held that **a convict's good conduct creates a presumption of rehabilitation** which then <u>imposes a burden on the state to rebut said presumption.</u> *Marra* held that the weight to be given to evidence of rehabilitation had to be exercised consonant with the two policies of:

1) Assisting in the convict's rehabilitation

2) Avoiding discrimination against the convict.

From the RECORD of the entire case, it is clear the RICO, DCCA and REC <u>could not and did not</u> rebut the presumption created by Travis "good conduct;" that Travis was, in fact, rehabilitated. Finally, the decision to revoke Travis' license does not assist in his rehabilitation -it only discriminates against him because of his conviction. *HRS section 831-3.1 3(d)* 's unambiguous language is clear. "... the state... or ... agencies <u>shall not take into consideration the conviction of any crime</u> except as provided by subsections (b) and (c)."

California law, for example, **mandates that a certificate of rehabilitation can prevent a person from being denied a license solely on the basis that he had been convicted of a felony.** So, too, with Hawaii. The agencies and courts abused their discretion by a failure to take into consideration the facts and law relating to *HRS section 831-3.1(a-d) and HRS 378-2 and 378-2.5,* and as a result there was an arbitrary and unreasonable departure from precedent and settled judicial custom.

Had the courts and agencies conducted an "[appropriate] investigation" pursuant to *HRS sec 831-3. 1 (3) and HRS 378-2 and 378-2.5* they would have found Travis had been "sufficiently rehabilitated to warrant the public trust."

The DCCA argues that there was no violation of due process in this case because (among other things) Travis was served with notice of the administrative disciplinary action and had an opportunity to present evidence. { AB@ 11} despite this claim, the DCCA shows nowhere in the Record that *HRS section 831-3. 1 (a-d)* was cited as a jurisdictional basis in this case.

> "A lack of jurisdiction over subject matter cannot be waived, so the question of jurisdiction is in order at any stage of the case." *Yamane v Pohlson*

As a consequence, because Travis was not on notice, Travis could not directly address the DCCA's failure to apply *HRS section 831-3.1 (a-d)*. This failure of notice deprived Travis of his due process rights. The REC's final order was issued in violation of due process. Travis received no notice that his rehabilitation was at issue. Due process consists of notice and an opportunity to be heard. Blacks -5th ed. P. 262 (1983). As a result Travis' rehabilitation was in play in order for the HO to make a relevant decision as to whether the agency of the REC had subject matter jurisdiction in this case. That is, the DCCA had the burden of proof to prove that Travis was somehow insufficiently rehabilitated for the REC to have subject matter jurisdiction which would allow it to revoke his license. Due to this lack of notice, Travis was prevented from presenting the relevant exhibits and /or testimony to put the

REC agency to its proper burden, nor was Travis on notice to request a continuance in order to submit the necessary proof.

Had Travis been put on **proper** notice, he would have taken steps to introduce the facts which are part of the **record** after the HO's recommended revocation of his license. Travis submitted letters from his federal probation officer which twice stated that his adjustment to supervised release was satisfactory. { D 45/ p 13-14} and that he had in fact completely satisfied all conditions of his supervisory release { D45/ p 81-83}. In addition, Travis submitted the release of the federal notice of lien which resulted from his paying all fines, penalties, costs of prosecution, costs of restitution and the payment of all federal taxes. { D45/p 15-15} Travis also submitted a letter stating that he had satisfied the federal thereputic requirement. { D45 p. 13-14} Travis even noted that he was currently undergoing self-initiated therapy to manage the high level of stress he was under as a result of his license being revoked. { D45/p.60}

Despite all of this subsequent **evidence,** the Circuit Court stated that the HO based his decision upon several factors, and that **Travis' rehabilitation was not the sole dispositive factor.** { TR: 11/18/11, p 19} It did this despite the argument that the HO only considered Travis' rehabilitation, if at all, collaterally, but not directly, as it should have been addressed under *HRS section 831-3. 1 (c) (3)* id. **"that the person so convicted has not been sufficiently rehabilitated to warrant the public trust."**

This is the law. The DCCA stated that as far as it knew, Travis had been released from federal prison and was in a halfway house. {TR: 11/18/11, p 20} The DCCA did not know if he was under supervised release. (id) *HRS section 831-3.1 (3).* **"for the purpose of this subsection, <u>such refusal suspension, or revocation may occur only</u> when the agency determines,**

AFTER INVESTIGATION

in accordance with chapter 9 1 . "

Pursuant to *HRS Section 91-14 (g)*, an administrative decision of mixed fact and law can <u>be overturned</u> due to the employment of an (3) unlawful procedure. The failure to put Travis on notice as to the threshold issue of rehabilitation which should have been raised via *HRS section 831-3.1 (a-d)* constitutes just such an unlawful procedure and requires that the revocation of Travis' license be overturned. This is the relief sought. Travis has suffered, due to the flagrant violation of the law by the aforementioned agencies and courts, extreme financial loss, the illegal loss of his real estate company that had been in business on Maui since 1982, the loss of his staff, the loss of his long established clients, the loss of reputation; Travis is facing foreclosure of his home of 25 years and his marriage of 40 years is weighing in the balance. Travis' health has suffered due to the extreme stress he has been subjected to and sees doctor's, specialists, physical therapists, et al on a regular basis. *HRS Section 91-14(g)(6)* states in relevant part, "that a court may reverse the REC's final order if appellant's substantial rights have been prejudiced because administrative conclusions are arbitrary and capricious or characterized by an abuse of discretion or are clearly an unwarranted exercise of discretion."

The **record** shows that Travis admitted to filing false (amended federal tax) documents (count 1) and pursuing legal actions against the federal government; specifically the Internal Revenue Service. (count 5) **Such legal authority as exists states that a conviction for such actions cannot form the basis for the revocation of a real estate license.** A non-Hawaii court has held that a state cannot revoke a real estate license because a licensee filed false federal income tax returns, *North Carolina Real Estate Licensing Board v Coe* , *198 S.E 2d 19 (1973)*

Even though the record shows the HO had before him a score of letters from Travis' former clients, friends, family and peers in the real estate industry which recognized Travis' honesty, integrity and fair dealings, the HO systematically abused his discretion as he failed to follow the *Yoshina* rule in granting the DCCA's motion for summary judgment by not viewing the letters in the "light most favorable to Travis. The DCCA noted that one legal standard involved was that articulated in *State Ex Rel v Yoshina,* *84 HAW 179, 932p. 2d 316 (1997)* whereby the HO was to determine the motion for summary judgment by viewing the facts presented in the light most favorable to Travis [d 43/ p 36] i.e. the actual letters exhibits A through Z (D43/p 73-117]. These letters stated that over a course of four decades of work, Travis had a sterling reputation of being both honest and truthful and this reputation survived his conviction. [id]

Texas law requires that a variety of factors such as the nature and seriousness of the crime, <u>the relationship of the crime to the purposes for requiring a license</u> to engage in the occupation, the amount of time since the person's last criminal activity, and <u>letters of recommendation</u> be taken into account even when the applicant has a felony. *Section. 213.28 Licensure of Persons With Criminal Offenses.* (emphasis added)

In the HO's findings of facts and conclusions of law IV <u>Recommended Order</u> he states: "...the hearing's officer has not been made aware of any prior complaints against respondent (Travis) in his capacity as a real estate broker and there is no indication on his record that his actions have led to consumer harm."

Travis has (had) been a licensed agent/broker since 1969. It appears the HO investigated Travis' record and history searching for violations but could find <u>none</u>. But when it came to investigating Travis' rehabilitation pursuant to the specific and mandatory law of *HRS sections 831-3.1 (a-d), HRS 378-2 and HRS Sec. 378-2.5* the HO was derelict in his ministerial duty to uphold the law by turning a blind eye and a deaf ear to Travis' complete rehabilitation.

A mandatory statute <u>requires</u> a specific course of action characterized by such directives as **"shall."** *HRS section 831-3.1(a-d) (a)* "a person **shall** <u>not</u> be disqualified from... em<u>ployment</u> by the state or any of its branches... agencies... solely by reason of a prior conviction of a crime." A mandatory provision in a statute is one the omission to follow which renders the proceedings to which it relates <u>VOID</u> ... it is also said that **when the provision of a statute is the essence of**

the thing to be done, it is <u>mandatory. Mandatory statutory provision is one which must be observed</u>." Blacks 6 ed. P. 962

According to the *National Employment Law Project (NELP)* approximately 70 million people in the United States, roughly one in every four adults have a criminal record that could compromise their ability to get a job. There is also ample data to show that unemployment is one of the driving forces behind recidivism or inmate re-incarceration, a leading factor in escalating prison costs across numerous states." Recidivism was brought up in the *Shimose* ruling.

While a number of law suits have been filed in recent years seeking to force major companies and even the federal government to change their disclosure policies in hiring, a growing number of state and local lawmakers are now also working to address the issue. Their efforts have come primarily through so called "fair chance" or "ban-the box" measures; the latter a reference to the box on many job applications where an applicant is asked to state if they have ever been convicted of a crime. In states with ban-the box laws, job applicants are not required to reveal their past criminal history in the initial phase of the hiring process, potentially giving them a better chance to show a potential employer their qualifications instead of being automatically removed from consideration. They are required to do so if they are selected for an interview or otherwise get past the initial screening. "The theory is that, if you let someone in that position get their foot in the door, the door that has always been shut now might just open" says Attorney Steven Lucfner of the New Jersey Ogletree, Deakins Law Firm which specializes in_employment law.

In 1998 Hawaii became the first state to adopt a statewide ban-the box law, and as stated before, the federal government in 2012 with the *United States Equal Opportunity Commission (EEOC)* issued guidelines removing the criminal_background question. Why then, after release from prison, on Travis' October 14, 2010 application for license(Exhibit_8_) was the person of Americorp International LLC required to answer question #5? Why was the question even there? "In the past **twenty** years (20), have you been convicted of a crime in which the conviction has not been annulled or expunged? "Why twenty 20 years? The instructions on the application are as follows: "Answer all questions circle the appropriate response. Questions 1 though 6 refer to the applicant, to any officer or director of the corporation ... or member of the LLC..."

The *Hawaii Civil Rights Commission Section 378-1* defines "person" as "one or more individuals, and includes, but is not limited to ... corporations... or the state, or any of its political subdivisions. *Section 378-2* **Discriminatory practices made unlawful.** Offenses defined. **It shall be an unlawful discriminatory practice** (1) because of.... **Arrest and Court Record** (b) for any employment agency to fail or refuse to refer for employment or classify or otherwise to discriminate against an individual.

The "Individual" "Person" of Americorp International LLC was discriminated against and was denied a real estate broker's license because of Travis' "Arrest and Court **Record"** and prior conviction. *HCRC Section 378-2.5 (B):* "An employer may inquire about and consider an individual's criminal conviction **record**... **provided that conviction record bears a rational relationship to the duties and responsibilities of the position."**

(c) "For purposes of the section, "conviction" pursuant to *Section 571-84*... provided that the employer may consider the employee's conviction record falling within a period that shall not exceed the most recent **10 years**..." the DCCA/REC application for license is in violation of the HCRC mandate of ten(10) years. Question #5 states." In the past twenty **(20) years** have you been convicted of a crime? Why was/is the state allowed to violate the mandate of the *Hawaii Civil Rights Commission?*

(d) Notwithstanding subsections (b) and (c), the requirement that inquiry into and consideration of a prospective employee's conviction record may take place only after the individual (person/ corporation/ LLC) has received a conditional job offer, and the limitation to the most recent ten (10) year period, excluding the period of incarceration, shall not apply to employers who are expressly permitted to inquire into an individuals criminal history for employment purposes pursuant to any federal or state law other than subsection(a) including

1) The state or any of its branches ... agencies pursuant to sections *78-2.7* and *Section 8313.1."* (Emphasis Added) Note that the *HCRC* references *HRS Section 831-3.1.* Is it possible that the members of the RICO, DCCA and REC are ignorant of the laws of Hawaii? Is

there any excuse for such ignorance of the law? Wouldn't the HO for the DCCA, a judge for the ICA, be aware of *HRS Sections 831-3.1(a-d) and HRS Section 378-2 and378-2.5?* This begs the question. Was the HO, the Chief Justice of the Intermediate Court of Appeals aware of the statute and deliberately hid it from Travis? Or, was he ignorant of the laws of the state of Hawaii? Black's 6th ed p. 746 "Ignorance. The want or absence of knowledge, unaware or uninformed. Ignorance of law is want of knowledge or acquaintance with the laws of the land in so far as they apply to the act, relation, duty, or matter under consideration...In criminal law, ignorance as to a fact may be a defense, but **ignorance as to law generally is no defense."** Was HO Craig Uyehara aware of HRS *Section 831-3.1(a-d) and 378-2 and 378-2.5* when it filed its motion for summary judgment? If so, why didn't he invoke it knowing it was the law of the land of Hawaii? He did not invoke it because if he had he would have had no case or cause to revoke Travis' real estate broker's license.

The license application for Travis/Americorp LLC was rejected prior to any revocation of Travis' real estate brokers license on April 29, 2011. The DCCA/REC is in violation of *HCRC section 378-2.5 (c) (d)* and pursuant to section 378-4 "the commission has jurisdiction over the subjects of discriminatory practices made unlawful by this part. Pursuant to subsection (d) the DCCA/REC could only inquire into Travis' conviction record "only after the individual has received a conditional job offer." Travis' application was rejected outright. The DCCA/REC should have followed the law and granted the license and then conduct their investigation pursuant to *HRS section 831-3 (a-d)*. *HCRC Section 378-2.5 (d) (1)* refers to *HRS section 8313.1*. The DCCA/REC could only reject Travis' application "after investigation" and could only revoke Travis license if pursuant to *HRS section 831-3.1* the *(b)* "the crime bears a rational relationship to the duties and responsibilities of the job " Travis has demonstrated beyond a shadow of a doubt that the DCCA/REC/RICO showed no such linkage between Travis' tax offenses and the duties of being a real estate broker.

The April 26, 2011 letter from Jon Ellis M. Pangilinan, [Exhibit 9] executive officer for the professional and vocational licensing division Department of Commerce and Consumer Affairs re: application for license real estate limited liability company states:

".... Therefore, after review of all the information presented at its December 16, 2010 monthly meeting, the real estate commission ("commission") denied your application for a real estate limited liability company license based on the following:

Section 467-8 prerequisites for license, registration or certificate.(a) no license, registration or certificate under this chapter shall be issued to:
(3) Any person who does not possess a reputation for or record of competency, honesty, truthfulness, financial integrity, and fair dealing.

Section 436 B-19 grounds for refusal to renew, reinstate or restore and for revocation, suspension, denial, or condition of licenses. In addition to any other acts or conditions provided by law, the licensing authority may refuse to renew, reinstate or restore or may deny, revoke, suspend, or condition in any manner, any license for any one or more of the following acts or conditions on the part of the licensee or the applicant there of:

(8) Failure to maintain a Record or history of, competency, trust worthiness, fair dealing, and financial integrity;…

(12) Failure to comply, observe, or adhere to any law in a manner such that the licensing authority deems the applicants or holder to be unfit or improper person to hold a license ….

This letter (April 26, 2011) amends our letter to you dated December 21, 2010, which incorrectly cites *HRS 467-14 (a) (3);* the correct citation is *HRS 467-8(a) (3).* Therefore, after review of all the information presented at its December 14, 2010, monthly meeting, the Real Estate Commission ("Commission") **denied** your application for a real estate limited liability company license. "

The hearings officer (HO) for the DCCA did not even make a recommended order until December 28, 2010 and the April 26, 2011 letter was two days before the REC voted to revoke Travis' license. Travis was guilty until proven innocent.

The REC was premature in its revocation. It had not conducted any investigation into Travis' rehabilitation and was barred by law from revoking Travis' license because the REC based the revocation on Travis' prior conviction. Because the issue of Travis' rehabilitation was not raised as an issue, Americorp's principal broker was not allowed to present evidence that Travis had been completely rehabilitated and worthy of the public trust. Again, Travis/Americorp International was denied due process of law. The REC completely violated the specific and mandatory statute of Hawaii revised statutes *(HRS) section 831-3.1* (a-d) and *HRS 378-2 and2.5.* Americorp International LLC's broker's license should never have been revoked

V CONCLUSION

1.   The legislative history of *HRS section 831-3.1* and its subsections *a-e* are a part of *Division 5 Title 38 Chapter 831,* a specific and mandatory statute which is favored, *Spirent,* id over the four general *Hawaii Revised Statutes* used as reason for revoking Travis broker's license. "The cardinal rule of statutory construction (is) that courts are bound to give effect to all parts of (the)statute and that no clause, sentence or word shall be construed as superfluous, void or insignificant if a construction can be legitimately found which will give force to and preserve all words of the statute." *State v Ortiz, 74 HAW343, 351-52, 845p 2d547, 551-52 (1993)* (citations omitted); see also *State v. Cummings, 101 Hawaii 139, 144-45 n.4, 63p. 3d 1109, 1114-15 n. 4 (2003); Coon v City and County of Honolulu, 98 Hawaii 233, 259, 47p. 3d 348, 374 (2002).*

P.2 of the ICA's summary disposition order dated December 17, 2014 erroneously states 1. "the commission had jurisdiction over Travis' license pursuant to *HRS Sections 26-9(b) (2009) 92-17 (b) (2012), 467-4 (2013), and 467-14(2013).* Travis' arguments regarding *HRS Section 831-3.1 (b)* (supp. 2013) do not deprive the jurisdiction of the commission to revoke a real estate broker's license." This is not the truth.

HRS 26-9 is a **general** statute which charged the REC with **protecting consumers.** The HO admits in his recommended order (HORO IV) "… the hearing's officer has not been made aware of any prior complaints against respondent (Travis) in his capacity as a real estate broker and there is **no indication on his record that his actions have led to consumer harm.**" Travis, in his entire four decades plus career has not harmed one consumer. "Whenever there is a conflict between a general and specific statute regarding the same subject matter, the specific is favored." *Spirint Holding Corp v State Dept. of Taxation.* Id

HRS 92-17 is a **general** statute which allowed the REC upon investigation to notify a licensee of proceedings against him. id. No Investigation pursuant to *HRS section 831-3.1 (a-d)* and *HRS 378-2 and378-2.5* and the issue of Travis' rehabilitation and a rational relationship between his offense and his job was made an issue.

The DCCA's position was that *HRS* Sec *-831-3.1* and all its subsections was "not in issue" and just brushed it off as if the specific mandatory statute was "superfluous, void, irrelevant and insignificant." All the DCCA could say in denial of the specific and mandatory statute was that "The Commission had jurisdiction to revoke Travis' license and that Travis' arguments regarding *HRS Section 831-3.1(a-d)* do not deprive the jurisdiction of the Commission to revoke a real estate broker's license." which flies in the face of the rule of statutory construction. The specific statute **does** "deprive the Commission jurisdiction."

The HO states: "HRS *Sec 467-4* allowed the REC to enforce *Chapter 467* and *HRS Sec. 467-14* allowed the REC to revoke a broker's license for **any cause authorized by law** "(Id). The DCCA, RICO, and REC pursuant to the unambiguous plain language of the mandatory specific statute *HRSSec.831-3.1 (a-d)* had no "cause authorized by law" to revoke Travis ' broker's license based on his prior conviction, complete rehabilitation and no rational relationship established between his tax offenses and the duties and responsibilities of being a real estate broker.

The ICA in their "summary disposition order" seriously erred in presenting the facts. Page 3 erroneously states: "...in light of *the evidence* that he intentionally **evaded** tax obligations over a few decades..." p 4. "...his **intentional evasion** of tax obligations over an **extensive** period of time.." is simply not the truth. (Exhibit 10-Indictment) 1)There was **no indictment for tax evasion.** The word "evasion" appears nowhere in the indictment. The **"false** tax returns" were amended returns pursuant to *IRC Section 1341(a)(1)(5)(A) (B);IRC of 1939 Chapter 1. Webster* defines **"false"** as "not accurate; in error; incorrect; wrong; mistaken: as a false argument." *New World p.524.*

2) **Absolutely no "evidence exists that Travis "intentionally evaded tax obligations".** 3) Travis did not file tax returns for 1996, 1997, 1998, 1999 and 2000. Five years does not represent "a few decades." "A few" means more than one. The ICA is saying "In light of the evidence." What evidence

does the ICA have that Travis evaded for even one year? Clearly the ICA has fabricated the information to make it seem like Travis has been evading taxes for over 30 years to cast him in an evil and dishonest light. This is dishonest.

The RICO, DCCA, and REC never once established that Travis' tax offenses were related to his job as a real estate broker. Not once. The **ONLY** way the DCCA/REC/RICO could have revoked Travis' license based on the prior conviction was a "rational" linkage that the offense was job related; i.e. Travis committed a crime related to real estate. If there were no consumer complaints against Travis in forty years it is hardly likely that Travis committed real estate crimes of any nature.

The only mention of the word "real estate" was on p. 3 of Exhibit 4. "The conclusions of law set forth as follows: [w]ith respect to *HRS 467-14(8)* (Travis) contends that his misguided protest of the tax laws does not amount to "fraudulent or dishonest dealings" relevant to **real estate transactions."** Where is the rational relationship between Travis' tax offences and "real estate transactions?" Where?

> 1) *Hawaii Revised Statutes (HRS) section 831-3.1 (2)* "... a person... convicted of a crime... that bears **a rational relationship to the duties of responsibilities of a job."**
> 2) *Hawaii Civil Rights Commission (HCRC) section 378-2 (2) (b)-* "...**provided that the conviction record bears a rational relationship to the duties and responsibilities of the position.**

3) *HRS Section 378-2.5 (a)* Subject to subsection (b), an employer may inquire about and consider an individual's criminal conviction record concerning hiring, termination, or the terms, conditions, or privileges of employment; **provided that the conviction record bears a rational relationship to the duties and responsibilities of the position.**

4) The *United States Equal Employment Opportunity Commission (EEOC)* -"employers cannot enact a blanket exclusion of persons convicted of any crime... unless the "employer can demonstrate **that the reason (of the crime) was job related."**

4. California law- a criminal record can affect one's application for a professional license only **if "the crime or act is substantially related to the qualifications and duties of the business or profession."**

5. *National Employment Law Project (NELP)*-One in every four adults in the United States have **a criminal record that could compromise their ability to get a job**...unemployment...behind recidivism or inmate reincarceration.."

6. "Texas law requires a variety of factors such as the nature and seriousness of the crime, **the relationship of the crime to the purposes for requiring a license to engage in the occupation..."** *Section 213.28: Licensure of persons with criminal offenses.*

7. *United States Civil Rights Act-"*... **where an employment policy of a state...that discriminates against criminal**s...employers **must show a business necessity** before 'automatically disqualifying criminals.'"

8. The *EEOC* guidelines say **employers should be able to show a nexus between any hiring restriction placed on felons and the jobs they are applying for.** Not doing so could open up the employer to civil rights litigation.

In the Shimose State Supreme Court ruling on January 16, 2015 the "HHSC/HMC failed to establish a rational relationship between Shimose's conviction and the duties and responsibilities of a radiological technician. When presented with cross- motions for summary judgment in the context of *HRS sections 378-2 and 378-2.5,* the court's task is two-fold. First the court must apprise itself of the undisputed material facts relating to the duties and responsibilities of the position. In so doing, the court is not necessarily limited to duties and responsibilities contained in a formal job description. Second, **the court must analyze the rationality of any relationship that the defendant has asserted between the conviction and the employee's ability to perform his or her undisputed job duties,**(emphasis added) Where factual issues bearing on the rationality of an asserted relationship remain, neither party is entitled to summary judgment."

The State of Hawaii Supreme court stated:"...A felony drug conviction simply has no bearing on an individual's ability to perform the primary imaging duties of a radtech at HMC. Accordingly, there is no rational relationship between Shimose's drug conviction and the core duties of a radtech at HMC that would have entitled HHSC/HMC to disqualify Shimose from prospective employment.(*14. Shimose argues that because he obtained licensure in radiology, his suitability for employment with HHSC/HMC cannot be questioned. However, the fact that an individual has received licensing and/or professional certification does not conclusively establish the absence of a rational relationship between a conviction and the duties and responsibilities of a position...)

In this case, HHSC/HMC **has not presented undisputed facts** (emphasis added throughout)**that establish a rational relationship** between a drug conviction and an HMC radtech's proximity to locked crash carts and drug reaction boxes...Furthermore, an HMC's radtech's potential access to the non-controlled substances contained in crash carts and drug reaction boxes **does not bear a rational relationship to a drug conviction**...Additionally, HHSC/HMC **failed to establish the rationality of the relationship between a drug conviction and an HMC's radtech's fitness to handle patient charts as a matter of law.** HHSC/HMC **failed to introduce undisputed material facts** showing that access to a patient's chart would lead to access to controlled substances...HHSC/HMC **did not introduce undisputed evidence** that its patients have physical control over controlled substances that might be diverted....HHSC/HMC merely asserted that there is a risk that vulnerable patients would have their medication taken. **In the absence of undisputed material facts** establishing access, HHSC/HMC WAS **NOT** ENTITLED TO SUMMARY JUDGMENT ON THIS THEORY (emphasis added).

Additionally, genuine issues of material fact remain regarding the asserted relationship between Shimose's felony conviction and the risk that vulnerable patients "might be sold an illegal drug."If *HRS Section 378-2.5* extended so broadly that any contact with elderly or young children created a rational relationship to a prior drug conviction, then all individuals with prior drug convictions could be disqualified from any job that dealt with the public at large. But **drug convictions often have nothing to do** with elder/child abuse, **and should not serve as a blanket disqualification from employment** that requires a modicum of interaction with children and the elderly. Such a broad discriminatory prohibition would contradict the legislative compromise of *HRS Section 378-2.5.*

IN CONCLUSION (Shimose)

"In conclusion, the circuit court erred when it granted HHSC/HMC's motion for summary judgment with respect to Shimose's statutory claim. Accordingly, we affirm in part and vacate in part the ICA's December 23, 2013 judgment on appeal and the circuit court's March 28, 2012 order granting HHSC/HMC's cross-motion for summary judgment, and remand to the circuit court for further proceedings consistent with this opinion."

The burden was on the RICO, DCCA and REC to prove Travis was not rehabilitated pursuant to *HRS section 831-3.1 (a-d) and HRS 378-2 and 2.5* and that there was a rational relationship between his tax offenses and his duties and responsibilities as the principal broker for Americorp International LLC. In blatant disregard of the law the RICO, DCCA and REC said Travis rehabilitation was "not an issue" and established absolutely no relationship whatsoever, rational or otherwise, that his tax offenses bore a rational relationship to his duties as a real estate broker. Travis was 100% rehabilitated and the RICO/DCCA/REC turned their backs on that material fact.

On p.3 of Exhibit 4 the ICA admits the basis of its decision to deny Travis' broker's license was his criminal conviction. "..The Conclusions of Law set forth in the hearing Officer's Findings of Fact and Conclusions of Law later adopted by the Commission, were as follows: [Travis] does not dispute that he failed to comply with the applicable tax laws that formed the basis for his criminal case..the undisputed evidence...(p.4) [Travis'] **CRIMINAL CONVICTION IS OF RECORD** and that **CONVICTION....**"

Petitioner Travis calls upon the State Supreme Court to award a Writ of Peremptory Mandamus in favor of petitioner Travis for all the reasons stated in this appeal, and grant relief to Travis and order the RICO, DCCA, REC to immediately reinstate Travis' real estate broker's license and the broker's license of his real estate company and allow him to seek relief pursuant to Petition for Declaratory Relief, *HRS Section 368-17;* punitive damages in civil actions brought under Part 1 of this chapter.

All the other issues raised by the DCCA/REC/RICO, Circuit Court and the ICA are moot based on *HRS 831-3.1(a-d), HRS Sec 378-2 and 2.5* and are not an issue in this case because they are based on the court record of Travis' prior conviction which contravenes the laws. The arguments need not be argued. The civil rights of Travis must be upheld. **The law pro-**

hibits the revocation of a license based on prior conviction and the ex-felon's rehabilitation.

If the DCCA/REC/RICO/Circuit Court and the ICA can prove Travis's offenses were related to his duties as principal broker for Americorp International LLC let them provide the evidence of those real estate related offenses and substantiate the revocation. The arguments made by the RICO/DCCA/REC/Circuit Court and ICA are not "cumulatively convincing" as they are not backed by the law of the land of Hawaii and the United States of America. For all the reasons stated above the Court should issue a Peremptory Writ of Mandamus in favor of Petitioner/Appellant/Travis.

Dated this March 20, 2015

www.ingramcontent.com/pod-product-compliance
Lightning Source LLC
Chambersburg PA
CBHW071534040426
42452CB00008B/1006